How Words Make Things Happen

How Words Make Things Happen

DAVID BROMWICH

OXFORD
UNIVERSITY PRESS

OXFORD
UNIVERSITY PRESS

Great Clarendon Street, Oxford, OX2 6DP,
United Kingdom

Oxford University Press is a department of the University of Oxford.
It furthers the University's objective of excellence in research, scholarship,
and education by publishing worldwide. Oxford is a registered trade mark of
Oxford University Press in the UK and in certain other countries

First Edition published in 2019

Impression: 1

Published in the United States of America by Oxford University Press
198 Madison Avenue, New York, NY 10016, United States of America

British Library Cataloguing in Publication Data
Data available

Library of Congress Control Number: 2018960359

ISBN 978–0–19–967279–0

Printed and bound in Great Britain by
Clays Ltd, Elcograf S.p.A.

To Edward Mendelson

Preface

This book is a revised and expanded version of the Clarendon Lectures that I gave in the Michaelmas term, 2013, at the University of Oxford. The topic grew out of a question that has puzzled me from the time I began to study literature. Every writer must have recognized the force of Yeats's declaration "Words alone are certain good." But what does the saying mean? Words drawn from thought and feeling, words composed without the direct stimulus of utilitarian purpose, may seem to stand clear of the mixed motives and compromises that belong to the world of action. Admit this uncontroversial fact, however, and immediately you are faced with a challenge.

Yeats meant to contrast a possible purity in words with the impurity of deeds. Yet words are valued because they move us, and who can say whether or when the thoughts they prompt will move us to *act*? Some of the writers who will be considered here (Burke, Lincoln) intended by words to affect the actions of their audience; others (Henry James, Yeats himself) appealed to thought and feeling without a pragmatic interest in changing the opinions of their readers. But no conceptual category, no enforceable distinction, can seal off language from its effects. To say it a different way: whatever an author may have meant, the consequences of language are not controlled by the author. This is one of the things we ought to mean by "the freedom of the writer," but it is apparently not something we want to mean. The admission of a necessary lack of control is sure to flatter neither the vanity of authors nor the self-respect of readers.

"The philosophers," wrote Marx in his Theses on Feuerbach, "have only *interpreted* the world in various ways; the point is to *change* it." He spoke as a revolutionist who saw the distance between the discovery of a true analysis of society and the will to act on it. This expression of doubt regarding the efficacy of persuasion ought to give us pause— coming, as it does, from an interpreter who would soon assist in composing one of the most demonstrably influential of political writings. Marx knew that every calculation of rhetoric assumes that persuasion can sometimes occur; but the assumption itself is surprisingly hard to prove. No doubt, people may come to think in ways they never thought before, but the cause may be a religious conversion, an intense friendship, a spell of sickness or anxiety—in short, many things besides a change of mind accomplished by words. All we can say about the transition is that something has changed in someone's beliefs.

Just as the attempt at persuasion may fail to persuade or may drag the reader in a direction unanticipated by the writer, so a literary production that aims at nothing but thought and feeling may find itself *doing* something, having an effect on the reader quite other than it imagined. This can be embarrassing to admit, in view of the more exalted claims that have been made for literature. "All values ultimately come from our judicial sentences," wrote Ezra Pound in a letter of 1922; and Geoffrey Hill in his essay "Our Word Is Our Bond" offered a necessary corrective: "In a poet's involvement with poetry, [there is] an element of helplessness, of being at the mercy of accidents, the prey of one's own presumptuous energy." Hill ended by approving a modified version of Pound's dictum: "All values ultimately go into our judicial sentences." But what do they do, once they are in there? And where do they go afterward?

Similar questions are prompted by Seamus Heaney's essay "The Government of the Tongue." The title itself is a pun that marks the author's ambivalence regarding the boundary between ideal and worldly authority. Heaney wanted to preserve a distinction between the imaginative and the persuasive uses of words, and yet he knew that such a distinction is difficult to sustain. The essay suggests a solution may come from "the idea that poetry vindicates itself through the exercise of its own expressive powers." Aesthetic rightness and rhetorical efficacy would thus be seen to coincide. But then, most strangely, Heaney chooses as an epitome of the self-vindication of poetry the passage of the Gospel of John about the woman taken in adultery.

The passage begins with the scribes and Pharisees citing the commandment which requires that the woman be stoned; they say this to tempt Jesus, "that they might have to accuse him." But Jesus "stooped down, and with his finger wrote on the ground, as though he heard them not." An attitude of unconcern and apparent detachment may have been useful for his survival, and it also goes with the lesson he means to impart: judge not, lest ye be judged. They prod him until he replies, "He that is without sin among you, let him first cast a stone at her"; at which the elusive stage direction is repeated: "And again he stooped down, and wrote on the ground." The men feel themselves to be "convicted by their own conscience," and they leave the scene, "one by one, beginning at the eldest, even unto the last." Jesus now raises himself and, seeing that he is alone with the woman, he asks, "Hath no man condemned thee?" She replies that none has. "Neither do I condemn thee: go, and sin no more."

The scribes and Pharisees evidently planned to accuse Jesus after hearing him utter a new law contrary to their own. He outwits them by saying nothing new, directing them instead to the universality of their law: it applies to each of them as much as to the woman. Heaney takes the passage to demonstrate the non-literal yet vast and unassailable powers that reside in poetry. But how does the activity of Jesus resemble the activity of a poet? "The drawing of those characters is like poetry," writes Heaney, "a break with the usual life but not an absconding from it." This seems a perverse emphasis. The writing by Jesus on the ground surely is an absconding if we consider it in isolation; whereas what happens afterward brings him into the common life. He saves the woman from being stoned to death by dispersing the crowd of her accusers. He does it by the force of his spoken challenge. But it is the undeciphered characters "written with his finger" that interest Heaney: "Poetry holds attention for a space [as Jesus does when he writes on the ground], functions not as distraction but as pure concentration, a focus where our power to concentrate is concentrated back on ourselves." This peculiar reading obeys an anomalous motive of twentieth-century defenses of literature. Words are at once praised for their ethical value and acquitted of the charge that they do something.

To repeat: the Gospel passage owes little of its force to the writing on the ground that Heaney associates with poetry. It is concerned with the world of action, the practical meaning of the law that Jesus publicly interprets in order to save the woman's life. Blake said that forgiveness of sins is the only teaching by which Christianity offers a moral principle distinct from the pagan philosophies. "There is not one Moral Virtue that Jesus inculcated but Plato & Cicero did inculcate before him. What then did Christ inculcate? Forgiveness of Sins.

This alone is the Gospel & this is the Life & Immortality brought to light by Jesus." This, too, is the doctrine promulgated by Jesus when he points to the universality of the law of forgiveness.

I have singled out Heaney and Hill because they were gifted writers who aimed to think clearly about the effects of words. The same perplexities occur when commentators of lesser stature address the subject. We are apt to treat with mockery, or with casual dismissal, the idea that poets are "unacknowledged legislators." But if we try to do justice to the influence of literature on life, we are fated to repeat the claim, in however disguised a form; and it looks as if Shelley was right after all: we cannot estimate what we owe to the unacknowledged (and unacknowledgable) legislators who affect us through language. A similar understanding applies to the everyday speakers of remembered words. Somebody is hearing them and getting a sensation that may hardly be discerned. Language affects human action, it is involved in almost everything we do, and its meanings are imperfectly determined, both ameliorated and degraded, by those who write and those who read. "Forgive them, for they know not what they do" in the present context may seem an excessive plea, but it is true enough that only partially and in the web of corrigible errors can we pretend to know what we are doing with words.

* * *

I should like to thank the Oxford Faculty of English for the invitation to deliver the Clarendon Lectures. The lectures are now called chapters, but I have not concealed indications that the book originated in talks to a diverse audience of scholars whom I hoped to convince by illustrative quotations of some length. The result is an extended essay, not a treatise, and I have kept the notes to a minimum by largely confining the references to quotations of two sentences or more. I have formalized the loose epistolary spelling in a letter by Burke, and punctuated the sentences above by Blake, but the commentary avoids anachronism by respecting the verbal habits of the authors in paraphrase as well as quotation. A final chapter, written later, is included here to underscore a warning against censorship which the preceding chapters may be felt to imply. Recent attempts to control the spread of dangerous language should be understood in the same light as all the other religious or moral codes that historically have sought to shelter human conduct from pollution by forces we cannot see, hear, smell, touch, or taste.

I am grateful to Seamus Perry for his warm hospitality and many kindnesses during my residence in Oxford, and for detailed comments which convinced me the argument was approaching the coherence I hoped for. I have profited from conversations with Sharon Achinstein, Matthew Bevis, Erica McAlpine, Timothy Michael, David Norbrook, Sophie Ratcliffe, and David Womersley. Harold Bloom gave an impetus to thoughts in this book that will continue beyond it. Georgann Witte read the manuscript at an early stage and contributed several improvements. Ross Borden read a late draft with his usual care, and I have followed many of his suggestions. Jacqueline Norton and Aimee Wright at Oxford University Press were most helpful on the way to publication, and Sarah Barrett's copy-editing strengthened the clarity and consistency of the text. "Spain" and "In Memory of W. B. Yeats" are quoted, in Chapter 4, with permission of the Estate of W. H. Auden. Chapter 5 is reprinted, with minor changes, from the *London Review of Books* (22 September 2016), and I thank the editors for their support.

Contents

Contents

The rhetorician would deceive his neighbours,
The sentimentalist himself.

—Yeats, *Ego Dominus Tuus*

Nothing will come of nothing: speak again.

—Shakespeare, *King Lear*

1

Does Persuasion Occur?

Austin, Aristotle, Cicero

I borrow the title of this series of lectures from two well-known phrases. W. H. Auden, in his elegy for William Butler Yeats, deplored the emotional extravagance and moral recklessness of the poet whose death he mourned, but he ended by granting a partial exoneration. Whatever Yeats's motives may have been, Auden declared, he could not be accused of fomenting wickedness, since, after all, "poetry makes nothing happen." This maxim was assimilated to critical doctrine in the 1950s and became part of the common sense of literary studies; and the defense of poetry it implies was still going strong a generation later, when one of my teachers, W. K. Wimsatt, memorably defined a poem as a verbal object whose only end is to be known. A poem, Wimsatt meant, isn't properly understood as the cause of effects worth looking into. A great poem shouldn't make you want to join a movement, or to change your life; its nature is not to persuade; and even if it has that effect on some people, that is not why it matters, not what we come to value it for. Think of readers of poetry who *are* affected so as to believe something—readers who believe so as to be convinced and possibly to act on their conviction—and you are thinking of untutored persons. They don't know how to take the words of a poem.

The other half of my title comes from J. L. Austin's book *How to Do Things with Words*. Though instruction on doing things with words may cut against the idea that words make nothing happen, Austin's sense of the way certain words perform specific actions was quite compatible with Auden's dictum that words of another sort reliably act so as to bring about no effect. Austin was not talking about poetry. Rather, his survey covered a limited set of verbal formulae that accomplish something concrete in the course of their saying or by virtue of certain words having been said. He mainly drew his examples from small and large ceremonial occasions: saying "Welcome" to people in order to welcome them, saying "Thank you" where the saying gives the thanks—so far, the point is so clear it may hardly need explaining. But we can easily call to mind interactions that have a more formal character. A policeman says to a culprit, "I arrest you," and in doing so arrests him; a priest affirms to a couple, "I now pronounce you man and wife," and they are married. It isn't hard to pick out the family resemblance among situations in which words either perform an action or constitute a necessary part of a performance in which their actual force is proved by the appropriate accompanying measures or gestures.

At first glance, the only *poems* that would seem to do this are poems in the shape of a preordained blessing or curse, a petition or prayer, such as Milton's sonnet "On the Late Massacre in Piedmont":

> Avenge O Lord thy slaughtered saints, whose bones
>   Lie scattered on the Alpine mountains cold,
>   Even them who kept thy truth so pure of old
>   When all our Fathers worshipped stocks and stones,
> Forget not.[1]

Milton's call for divine retribution against the killers of the Waldensian heretics is inseparable from the prayer-like command, *Avenge!* But God is not his only listener. Remembrance, so far as it can be performed, turns into a fact through the utterance of the imperative *Forget not!* For a less weighty instance, compare Tennyson's affirmation in his lovely verses "To E. FitzGerald" that the poem he is writing will itself be his appropriate gift: "And so I send a birthday line / Of greeting." He knows that his old friend will welcome the special gift in accordance with the pattern of their friendship,

> When, in our younger London days,
> You found some merit in my rhymes,
> And I more pleasure in your praise.[2]

The words both anticipate and prove the continuity of a reciprocal feeling.

Contemporary theorists of textual interpretation have shown considerable interest in Austin's idea of the "performative utterance." I have in mind particularly the writings of Quentin Skinner and

J. G. A. Pocock, which interpret texts in the canon of political thought as speech acts directed to a certain audience at a certain time. The readers of a persuasive text, it is argued, learn how to read the verbal cues in a special and almost-explicit way; persuasion, on this view, functions so that the reader completes a performance intended by the writer. My argument takes a similar starting point without trying to establish a set of generic constraints or allusive signals that open a path of communication between writer and reader. I am concerned rather with occasions on which words may persuade in spite of themselves, and often in spite of their avowed intention.

Anyone who has ever been asked to prove that persuasion occurs will realize how hard it is to take the first steps in such a proof. I found this out in my first years of teaching, when a colleague in the philosophy department denied that people's minds were ever changed by the things other people said. I thought the opposite was true and cited the example of Martin Luther King—hadn't King changed the minds of a great many people? The philosopher denied it. He made no pretense of having mastered any sociological or political data that could shed light on the case. On theoretical grounds alone, he simply did not believe that minds could be changed by words. My response, that there were people who *testified* to the impact of King's speeches, failed to settle the dispute.

I recall this deadlock partly as a warning about the readings that support my argument. No words can suffice as proof of the consequences of words. The very idea of persuasion is metaphorical—it supposes a bridge between two minds—and on this ground, a literalist can always stop you short. But I am interested in the half-metaphorical, half-literal usages that mark a boundary between rhetoric and poetry, or between the persuasive and the imaginative uses of words—a boundary we generally acknowledge to exist while recognizing that it is exceedingly difficult to locate. I will ask what it is about an attempted act of persuasion—and, in the minds of some readers, a demonstrably successful act—that makes it so hard for us say for sure whether the words are fanciful or accurate, fictional or matter-of-fact, plainly false or manifestly true. Persuasive words may be both things, of course—they may be at once fanciful and true—but they don't show their colors with a satisfying clarity one way or the other. Allowing for this necessary qualification, I proceed on the assumption

that persuasion does occur, and that we can know it does by introspection, even if we heed no other testimony. At the same time, the
results of a given attempt at persuasion are uncontrollable. It is easier
to say that certain words *will* affect people than it is to say *how* the
words will affect them.

* * *

Consider an extreme example of persuasion that was probably
unintended. Near the end of *A Letter to a Noble Lord,* Edmund Burke
imagines with sensational vividness the demolition of the landed
estates of his enemy and detractor the duke of Bedford. Burke
supposes the agents of destruction to be the French Jacobins who
will have invaded and conquered England—an action the radical
politics of the young duke might be taken to have encouraged. The
passage begins, "His Grace's landed possessions are irresistibly invit-
ing to an *agrarian* experiment"; and the phantasmagoria that unrolls
must have seemed to Burke's followers a brilliant vindication of his
counter-revolutionary argument, a deserved satire on the dangerous
pretensions of men of privilege who "commit waste on the inheritance." Yet we know that the same passage was capable of having a
different effect. To Romantic radicals of the next generation such as
the young William Hazlitt, it exemplified the ascendancy of individual genius over inherited power and privilege. Burke was uttering
fearless truths against the unmerited distinction of aristocracy; whatever his intention may have been, one effect of the *Letter* was to
undermine the pretensions of the nobility. *A Letter to a Noble Lord* is
a satirical polemic with an overtly political subject; it would now be
classified (in the crudest terms) as non-fiction; but that helps very
little in gauging the consequences of Burke's imaginings. Even a
proper generic "frame" cannot prevent a response that goes aslant
of anything the author intended. Words act in divergent ways on
intelligent readers.

Consider now a quite different example from the art of fiction.
Henry James in his novels and stories drew many portraits of the
"collector," the man (it is usually a man) who exhibits a wonderful
curatorial concern with his impressions, or with his acquisition of rare
or delicate objects. There is likely to be some initial agreement on
which characters we judge to be specimens of the type. Gilbert Osmond

in *The Portrait of a Lady* is one; another is the nameless "publishing scoundrel" of *The Aspern Papers*. But subsequent disagreement may cover a wide range. How do we judge the moral character of Adam Verver in *The Golden Bowl?* The answer will depend in large measure on what we make of his relationship to his daughter, Maggie, a relationship that borders on the incestuous. When the two of them manipulate their respective partners in order to restore the integrity of Maggie's marriage, their secret intimacy outweighs the love they feel for their mates. This will appear to some tastes perverse, to others a transubstantiation of love to a higher register. Our judgment necessarily brings into play many things about *us*, quite apart from on our grasp of what James wanted us to think—even if we could be sure what he was aiming at in *The Golden Bowl*. In a case like this, the dispute about meaning turns us back to irreducible intuitions about "how to live and what to do," the actions we admire and the things we care for most.

And the causes we are willing to fight for. Thoreau's great essay "Civil Disobedience" was credited by Gandhi with having exerted a major influence on his thought; among the few other writings he placed in the same category was Ruskin's *Unto This Last*. Thoreau, who said the hanging of John Brown, the anti-slavery terrorist, would "make the gallows as glorious as the cross," and Ruskin, the feudal critic of high capitalism, would have been equally surprised at their offspring: a doctrine and practice of non-violent resistance that ended British rule in India. The uncontrollability of persuasion, however, doesn't come under the heading of ambiguity; though the two are related, they indicate separate kinds of uncertainty. An ambiguity, even if unconscious on the part of the author, must have been *allowed for* by the author. It picks up plausibility from the words themselves and from something about the nature of the work: the relevant context being taken into account, we decide that the words invite an ambiguous reading. By contrast, the unanticipated consequences or vagrant by-products of persuasion may interest us most intensely when they counteract the author's evident wish. When, in short, they give the reader something more or something other than the author bargained for.

Persuasion is a necessary word no doubt, but dull and rather ungainly as it is commonly used. We bring it into sharper focus if we think of tracking a possible conversion of the reader to a definite belief.

But this is not exactly a case of belief *in*, as we would say of a subscriber to a settled doctrine, nor is it a case of belief *that*, as we would say of a proposition about the world that can be put into an indicative sentence. There is a subtler understanding about belief that I think powerful writers and speakers share, whether they know it or not.

* * *

Man is a believing animal. It is human to *want* to believe things, and a hunger for belief drives much of human conduct. This fact alone explains much of the content of religion and politics, and a good deal of the interest in works of the imagination that we recognize as bringing with them no practical directive. I would distinguish the hunger for belief from what William James called "the will to believe," by which he meant the desire for a solid faith in which to ground our most consequential actions. James was pointing to a source of the conviction that we possess freedom of the will, a source that would allow us to anchor that feeling in something greater than ourselves. I am describing something much less available to conscious awareness: an eager readiness for contact with apparent realities, but a readiness that doesn't involve credence or the putting a proposition into practice. Think of the common expression "You're kidding!" When we say it in a certain way, closer to laughter than alarm, we always mean the same thing: "I hope it's true—but true or not, how lucky to be hearing of anything so fascinating and improbable." *You're kidding*: we like it best if the thing is true but (so great is our hunger for belief) we give the speaker credit even if he or she was putting us on. The joke was on us, and it is almost as good as if it were true. We treat as a manifestation of *wit* the recounting of a possibly true story and, equally, a successful lie which we find gripping. That must have been one reason why Aristotle in his *Rhetoric* defined wit as "well-bred insolence." Suppose a speaker has embarrassed us by eliciting our belief in a lie. What of it? The belief itself still interests us and we pardon the trespass. Skepticism, which alongside curiosity is the parent of science, is a late development in human nature.

Believing, however, is only half the puzzle. In a few persons, whose importance is out of proportion to their share of the human group, there is a hunger to be believed. I tell you a story, maybe a true story, because I want you to hear it approvingly; and the sure sign of your approval will be your belief. The pressing desire to be believed—so I will argue in the second lecture—is a source of our fascination with dramatic soliloquies that exhibit in detail the process of rationalization or self-justification. We can see the same desire at work in the search for explanations that look toward first-person action. When we are hard at work persuading ourselves, we talk to ourselves silently; but this inward dialogue follows none of the protocols of empirical prudence or disinterested morality; it may ignore even the demands of simple self-interest. In such deliberations, we see *ourselves* as people who want to be believed. Of all the great novelists, Henry James excelled in the portrayal of a consciousness that is at once the subject and the object of a hunger for belief.

Following the treatment, in the first two lectures, of persuasion, action, and belief in general, and of speakers who convince themselves, such as Shakespeare's Brutus and Milton's Satan, the third lecture aims to illustrate a similar process but now involving a high degree theatrical artifice and premeditation. Here, the speaker appeals to an audience from explicit knowledge of their common situation, and the performance inseparably mixes logical, ethical, and emotional lines of address. In pursuing this topic, unlike the others, I will stay mostly within the bounds of rhetorical analysis properly speaking. Even here, the analysis will show, there are possible inferences from a well-plotted speech that would startle the speaker who saw them beforehand. This is a general truth about words that excite us, and a truth certainly known to the ancients: no tears in the speaker, no tears in the listener. Horace also expected us to know that tears affect us most when they come unbidden.

The fourth lecture deals with the difficulty of applying our usual canons of responsibility to a poem that works like an oration or a formal apology, a poem that is in fact working to convince itself and its readers of a practical truth it cannot bear to specify. When John Stuart Mill said that "eloquence is *heard*, poetry is *over*heard," he made no allowance for those occasions when a poet talks himself into an impassioned and influential attitude on a public question, and consents to be overheard by readers while he does so. The practical influence of a literary work, as the cause of an effect that goes beyond attitude, may call into question our usual ideas about "aesthetic distance" and the separation between the aesthetic and the ethical.

We may find it hard to avoid the conclusion that the artist has *done* something wrong with words.

* * *

When language is both imaginative and persuasive, its meanings can't be confined within the limits that grammarians and critics like to set. This may still be the case when we are intensely conscious of our wish to control the range of our meanings. Burke's *Enquiry into the Sublime and Beautiful* compares a verbal description to a painting in order to convince us that the painting, just because it produces visible effects, is less effective than words at raising strong emotions. Words are superior paradoxically, says Burke, because they yield a more obscure image of their object; they therefore leave more to the imagination; they are better suited to feeding the passions for the very reason that they have a harder time approaching clarity and truth. The discussion occurs in a section of the *Enquiry* where Burke draws heavily on Longinus, a section often remembered for the aphorism "we yield to sympathy what we refuse to description." But even a verbal description on this view wants to be picture-like: it is trying for sharp definition and that is the problem (the problem, I mean, for someone interested in raising strong emotions). Draw out the observation a little further and Burke will seem to be implying that great effects are incompatible with any stretch of words that pleases too much by being merely accountable.

In fact, Burke makes an inference still more radical when he resumes the comparison of word and picture in the final part of the *Enquiry*. Here his declared subject is "Words." We rely on words as universals, he says, and so thoroughgoing is this reliance that words may shed all pretense of referring precisely to anything. On this account, the passage from designation to abstraction is hardly conscious. The frequent failure of words to deliver the literal value they promise, or the literal help we wrongly expect of them, turns out to be a perverse convenience for the imagination. "The sounds being often used without reference to any particular occasion, and carrying still their first impression, they at last utterly lose their connection with the particular occasions that gave rise to them." The gradual process of dissociation over time, which turns apt metaphors into dead metaphors, works also to turn referring into non-referring literalisms. I called it a perverse convenience but it is also an ordinary convenience to be forever sending and receiving the approximate signals that form our linguistic currency. We feel no cause for alarm since it is open to us to check the worth of the signals by other means—detectable tones of voice, acquaintance with the speaker, and so on.

"Nothing"—this is more from Burke on words —"is an imitation further than as it resembles some other thing; and words undoubtedly have no sort of resemblance to the ideas for which they stand." Just because words are unmeaning in this sense, they are well fitted to convey a strong charge of irregular passion. So we yield ourselves to the sympathy evoked by words; we yield for better and also for worse. But a master of persuasion who recognizes this truth must accept the uncertainty of success in achieving a *desired* effect from words. Burke, in his own rhetorical practice, was particularly anxious about that uncertainty, and in his *Speech on Fox's East India Bill*, in the middle of his attack on the commercial empire of the East India Company, he paused to wonder at the way a vivid description of cruelty might counteract the proper effects of sympathy:

> It has been said (and, with regard to one of them, with truth) that Tacitus and Machiavel, by their cold way of relating enormous crimes, have in some sort appeared not to disapprove them; that they seem a sort of professors of the art of tyranny, and that they corrupt the minds of their readers, by not expressing the detestation and horror that naturally belong to horrible and detestable proceedings.[3]

Strong disapproval does attach to such crimes, as we experience or witness them; but owing to the uncertainty of words and our non-moral curiosity regarding new objects, the natural operation of the emotions is suspended when fascinating atrocities are impartially recounted. We do not know quite what we are feeling then.

One can find a related thought in Burke's letter of November 1789 to Charles-Jean-François Depont—the letter that was the germ of *Reflections on the Revolution in France*. Burke had hesitated to send it, he tells his young correspondent in France, because "in seasons of jealousy, suspicion is vigilant and active," and if the authorities intercepted the letter they might piece together indications that could be used against its recipient.

> In the ill connected and inconclusive logic of the passions, whatever
> may appear blamable, is easily transferred from the guilty writer to the
> innocent receiver. It is an awkward, as well as unpleasant accident; but
> it is one that has sometimes happened. A man may be made a martyr to
> tenets the most opposite to his own.[4]

This is prudent advice, and the matter might seem to end with the
warning to take care. But coming from an author who had written
earlier and emphatically of the non-resemblance between words and
ideas, Burke's excuse for the delay in sending his message implies a
more general warning. A writer—any writer—may be made the cause
of conversions he did not intend. A *work* may be made a martyr to
purposes the most opposite to those it declares on its face—and this,
not from any lack of competence in delivering an esoteric message, but
rather because of the fallibility of persuasion itself.

Such skepticism about the intended path and the actual destination
of words is not a modern discovery. It was known to Longinus as well
as Burke; and Cicero seems aware of the danger when in *De Oratore* he
cites Demosthenes on the most important parts of an oration: delivery,
delivery, and delivery. He means that you can always make the same
words mean different things. Still, it is relatively rare for scholars of
rhetoric to keep their eyes fixed on this uncertainty. From the eighteenth century through the early twentieth, it was widely, though not
universally, supposed that poetry should accomplish something definite and controllable, with assured effects of the sort I am suggesting
rhetoric can never obtain.

You find this assumption in some unlikely places. G. Lowes Dickinson,
in *The Greek View of Life,* spoke for just such a rational didactic result
when discussing the effects of catharsis on the audience of Greek tragedies. It worked, he thought, like a repeatable conversion that carried
people from one state of mind to another:

> Melody, rhythm, gesture and words, were all consciously adapted to
> the production of a single precisely conceived emotional effect; the
> listener was in a position clearly to understand and appraise the value
> of the mood excited in him; instead of being exhausted and confused by
> a chaos of vague and conflicting emotion he had the sense of relief
> which accompanies the deliverance of a definite passion, and returned
> to his ordinary business "purged," as they said, and tranquilized, by a

process which he understood, directed to an end of which he approved.[5]

Notice the emphasis here on "deliverance" of a definite passion—which must mean at once being allowed to experience a great and piercing emotion and being relieved of a dangerous and intolerable emotion.

Aristophanes in *The Frogs* doubted the efficacy of any such attempted ameliorative therapy in the arts. The Dionysius of that satire judges a contest between the best lines offered by Euripides and Aeschylus. Euripides puts forward the sentence: "Skill in speech is Persuasion's inner shrine." Aeschylus responds: "Death is the sole god who cannot be bought." When Dionysius pronounces Aeschylus the winner, Euripides is baffled. What did he do wrong? Dionysus answers that Aeschylus won because "he threw in Death, the heaviest of evils." But, says Euripides, "I threw in Persuasion, and made an adorable verse." Dionysus settles the argument with a warning: "Persuasion's a tricky, bodiless affair. Come, look through your plays, you must find something solid."[6] And it's true, persuasion is a tricky and bodiless affair.

* * *

Common sense affords a clear enough idea of our reasons for using words to communicate: we want to be sociable and to be understood. Reductionist accounts of meaning come from supposing that those reasons explain more than they do. An author, it is said, produces words that intend a certain sense and effect; a reader, of the sort the author had in view, understands and rightly interprets those words; and their sense is approved or admired in accordance with that understanding. Words are thereby used to satisfy an implicit contract, an agreement on the terms of proper understanding, which author and reader might both recognize if it were once spelled out. The great biographical critics in English, Johnson and Ruskin among them, show throughout their practice what an impressive hold this picture exerted on readers of the eighteenth and nineteenth centuries.

This view of the purposive adequacy of language derives ultimately from Aristotle's *Rhetoric*. Persuasion is valued there for its conveyance of "situated judgment" and "deliberative partiality"—I borrow the phrases from Bryan Garsten's excellent study of rhetoric in political thought, *Saving Persuasion*. Aristotle believed that rhetoric "could be a technical art of deliberation," writes Garsten, "insofar as it studied the internal structure of public opinion, looking for deliberative pathways between various beliefs and emotions."[7] The *Rhetoric* describes four such pathways an orator may follow to plant conviction in his listeners.

There is an ethical appeal, which relates to the stature and morale of the speaker, and there is an affective appeal, which bears on the accessible emotions of his listeners. Also on Aristotle's list are valid argument and apparent argument (that is, an extended false inference or a lie skillfully told). The generous final category, apparent argument, can accommodate the delivery of an insincere but expected comfort by the speaker, understood as the speaker does or as he doesn't want it to be understood. Of course there is another possibility. The speaker may not know exactly where he stands, and his words may expose his ethical posture more vividly than he realizes.

This last is a sort of performative situation that should have interested J. L. Austin; and in fact it drew from him a discerning comment in his essay "Performative Utterances": "If I say 'I congratulate you' when I'm not pleased or when I don't believe that the credit was yours, then there is insincerity."[8] Irony, too, may lurk in this deliberative pathway, an irony that steals upon the speaker: "I didn't mean it that way." (But he said it like that because part of him did mean it.) Again, a routine acknowledgment of an achievement I am not moved by can take on an undertone of contempt. There are after-dinner speeches and wedding toasts that skirt a limit of transparent hyperbole or insincerity. Our words are tools, according to Austin; but sometimes they undermine with a pick-axe where they meant to lay on with a trowel.

Austin came closer to grappling with such possibilities in another passage about performative deviations that cannot be classified as misfires:

> I may say "I welcome you," bidding you welcome to my home or whatever it may be, but then I proceed to treat you as though you were exceedingly unwelcome. In this case the procedure of saying "I welcome you" has been abused in a way rather different from that of simple insincerity.[9]

But my behavior subsequent to asking you in may give a true (though involuntary) reflection of my feelings and not just an abuse of the convention of welcoming. And some of my subsequent behavior may be in words.

A last pertinent example, from Austin again on performative utterances:

> In using the imperative [*Shut the door*] we may be ordering you to shut the door, but it just isn't made clear whether we are ordering you or entreating you or imploring you or beseeching you or inciting you or tempting you, or one or another of many other subtly different acts which, in an unsophisticated primitive language, are very likely not yet discriminated.[10]

I can say "Shut the door" emphasizing *shut* to mean not just halfway; or emphasizing *door* to indicate that I already told you once. I can say it going down the scale to register exasperation; or going up the scale to end in a meek question and polite pleading to a loved one. One can even imagine the sentence said in a rules-of-the-house flat monotone—this to be reserved, perhaps, for a person in dealing with whom tact is not essential, or for use at a plainly exigent moment (I may be carrying a heavy box and under obvious strain). Expression works up the necessary discriminations to create a refined rather than a primitive language, in the terms given by Austin's argument; but in any extended rhetorical representation that bears a purpose, all the words and tones of voice around the action-imperative lend a shading to what is said; and those modifications in turn affect the meaning of the imperative.

Austin started from a premise that his book *How to Do Things with Words* could have taken from Aristotle's *Rhetoric*: we can describe and catalogue the uses of persuasive words in much the way we write natural history, since the actions and events in question look to attain a particular result by calculations of probability. It is a sensible premise, with which I agree, and I will begin therefore by assuming the utility of a similar behaviorist approach to linguistic surface. Words are always adequate before they are more than adequate. "The one thing we must not suppose," writes Austin, " is that what is needed in addition to the saying of the words [in a performative utterance] is the performance of some internal spiritual act, of which the words then are to be the report."[11] The saying is itself the act. It is not a description of an act. This was accepted doctrine, too, among the advanced literary critics of the 1940s and 1950s—William Empson, R. P. Blackmur, Kenneth Burke—who published many of their best-known interpretations and theoretical papers at the time when Austin was doing his major work. Yet Austin is so minimally academic a writer that it is impossible to guess whether he was aware of the affinity.

Pressed to define more closely what he was up to, Austin in "A Plea for Excuses" called his researches "linguistic phenomenology," and explained himself thus:

> Our common stock of words embodies all the distinctions men have found worth drawing, and the connexions they have found worth marking, in the lifetimes of many generations: these surely are likely to be more numerous, more sound, since they have stood up to the long test of the survival of the fittest, and more subtle, at least in all ordinary and reasonably practical matters, than any that you or I are likely to think up in our arm-chairs of an afternoon.[12]

I do not share the optimism (about language and perhaps some other things) which comes out in his reference to the survival of the fittest. Still, linguistic uses that are time-worn and time-honored may be supposed to have some worth today, if they were worth saving yesterday. These tools provide "equipment for living," as Kenneth Burke called them, but it can sometimes seem that the tools have a life of their own. "Should we say, are we saying," Austin writes, "that he took her money, or that he robbed her? That he knocked a ball into a hole, or that he sank a putt? That he said 'Done', or that he accepted an offer? How far, that is, are motives, intentions and conventions to be part of the description of actions?"[13] All these descriptions are tags that can be shown to be rightly or wrongly placed. But that only holds true so long as we are concerned with the commonest of conventional actions. "He took her money" may mean that he robbed her, when for example we are describing a hustler or a contriver of a Ponzi scheme—when, that is, our description has reference to the qualities of an agent or action. But to a great extent, words themselves—the minute distinctions between expressions as closely adjacent as Austin's examples—are the best evidence we have of intentions at odds with avowed motives. Conventional meanings may be dislodged by the pressure placed on a conventional expression; and so an act of persuasion often drives beyond a speaker's conscious will. This may have been the case, as we shall see, with Abraham Lincoln's use of the phrase "I do not expect," concerning the possibility of civil war in 1858. "Hope," "predict," "expect" are borderline performative words; and of them all, "expect" is the most susceptible to irony, just because it is the most neutral-seeming.

*   *   *

Can words—can the history of a habit of using words in a certain way—*cause* their intention to be rightly construed? Austin's most penetrating look at this challenge comes in a passage of "A Plea for Excuses" that deals with the idea of causation itself.

> "Causing," I suppose, was a notion taken from a man's own experience of doing simple actions, and by primitive man every event was construed in terms of this model: every event has a cause, that is, every event is an action done by somebody—if not by a man, then by a quasi-man, a spirit. When, later, events which are *not* actions are realized to be such, we still say that they must be "caused", and the word snares us: we are struggling to ascribe to it a new, unanthropomorphic meaning, yet constantly, in searching for its analysis, we unearth and incorporate the lineaments of the ancient model.[14]

So, it would seem, the genealogy of usage brings us close to a genealogy of illusions. We are in the habit, which belongs to the conditions of our nature, of making coherence out of a story that may not on its face promise comprehension or even offer much coherence. But in literature as in common experience, something in us wants to take the word for the deed. Accordingly, we take the thing that the word says it is for the word's sufficient sense. We may even do so when the feelings that the word evokes are telling us something quite different.

The ordinary idea of persuasion, to repeat, asks us to presume a speaker and a listener brought into accord by an adequate expression. A very different picture of communication between speaker and listener, or between author and reader, emerges from Donald Davidson's essay "A Nice Derangement of Epitaphs":

> The interpreter comes to the occasion of utterance armed with a theory that tells him (or so he believes) what an arbitrary utterance of the speaker means. The speaker then says something with the intention that it will be interpreted in a certain way, and the expectation that it will be

so interpreted. In fact this way is not provided for by the interpreter's theory. But the speaker is nevertheless understood; the interpreter adjusts his theory so that it yields the speaker's intended interpretation. The speaker has "gotten away with it."[15]

The idea of transparent conveyance of meaning has here been surrendered, but the desired result, a mutually agreeable understanding, is retained on other terms. This is felt to be sufficient because it can be checked by later communications between the same speakers. Davidson leaves room for the sort of ambiguity between intention and understanding that Austin showed little interest in. But the idea of an after-check doesn't help much, after all, in reading imaginative works, where we are given just one set of signals to mark the cumulative contact between reader and author. It is a comparatively unusual experience to reread an author and find him saying yes where we thought he must be saying no. And yet it does happen. Interpretations of literature in any case issue from a single extended and always deepening impression, and not from discrete acts of reading that we can regard as separate events.

An author's attempt to convey a powerful feeling, whether in the form of a named passion such as indignation or a not yet namable passion, may carry a new effect into the world. Any true account of such effects must allow for an element that evades the understanding, the quality that makes it impossible to say in response to a work of literature: "I agree." Plato, who saw this truth about writing, asked in the *Phaedrus* why the words of the great poets and orators, if you question them, "maintain a solemn silence." Words, he concluded, that come to us finished and framed should never be trusted, since they are both mystifying and irresponsible:

> If you ask them anything about what they are saying, if you wish an explanation, they go on telling you the same thing, over and over forever. Once a thing is put in writing it rolls about all over the place, falling into the hands of those who have no concern with it just as easily as under the notice of those who comprehend; it has no notion of whom to address or whom to avoid.[16]

In the same dialogue, Socrates compares this defect of rhetoric with the virtuous readiness-in-reply of the masters of dialectic—"a discourse which is inscribed with genuine knowledge in the soul of the learner; a discourse that can defend itself and knows to whom it should speak and before whom to remain silent." By contrast with dialectic, rhetoric is literally arrogant: it arrogates a privilege to itself, presumes the nature of the question under discussion, and shrugs off any justification of its procedures. Plato was working to combat the prestige of sophists, lawyers, and demagogues, as well as poets. Most of all he was interested in denying their claim of knowledge.

It was in response to this challenge that Cicero in *De Oratore* chose not to praise the linguistic dexterity but rather the civic virtuosity and responsiveness that might be encompassed only by the orator. According to the younger participants in that dialogue—and they can cite for corroboration the fame of the speaker they most admire, Crassus— the orator stands to the city in roughly the relation we may suppose a conductor stands to an orchestra, or a gifted parliamentary leader to the party in whose ranks he rose. The interlocutor of Crassus in this dialogue is Antonius, a civic-minded worker in the Roman courts of law, who offers no such analogy but simply lists the desired attributes:

> In an orator we must demand the subtlety of the logician, the thoughts
> of the philosopher, a diction almost poetic, a lawyer's memory, a
> tragedian's voice, and the bearing almost of the consummate actor.[17]

The quality of endless versatility that threw doubt on the claims of the rhapsode in Plato's *Ion* is turned to advantage in this characterization of the orator. We are not asked to think twice about the person who masters the verbal costume of every craft while acquiring the knowledge of none. When deployed in the cause of civic virtue, dexterity with language becomes an unmixed good.

We are given to understand that Antonius excels at the lower forensic oratory of the courts. When subjected to his honest scrutiny, the metaphors deployed by Crassus, the grand public man, are shown to be buried metaphors uncomfortably close to cliché; and under the glare of interrogative challenge, the trite figures of speech wither and retreat into non-meaning.

> "Deliver us out of our woes, deliver us out of the jaws of those whose
> ferocity cannot get its fill of our blood; suffer us not to be in bondage to
> any, save to yourselves as a nation, whose slaves we can and ought to
> be." I pass over "woes," in which, according to the philosophers, the
> brave can never become involved; I pass over "jaws," out of which you

> desire to be delivered, for fear of your blood being sucked out of you by
> an unjust judgment, a thing which they say cannot befall the wise; but
> "slavery," did you dare to say that not yourself only, but the entire
> Senate, whose interests you were that day upholding, could be slaves?[18]

Notice what has happened. The call for deliverance led naturally to
the most lurid answer to the question, *Deliverance from what?* What
indeed, if not the jaws of a predatory beast? The careless but service-
able trope cleared the way to impute a slavish disposition to anyone
who would submit; for people must have become slaves already, or
must stand in peril of sinking under the thrall of dictatorship, if they
can never be summoned except by the call of an inspired orator. And
yet it is conscious republicans, of all people, who shouldn't be lightly
characterized as slaves; and statesmen who think their lives mortgaged
to the public trust should not be supposed to suffer woes from the
prospect of a temporary failure.

Antonius goes a step further in his interrogation of the stock figures:

> Can Virtue be a slave, Crassus, according to those authorities of
> yours, whose maxims you include within the range of the orator's
> knowledge? ... And as for your further pronouncement, that the
> Senate not only "can" but actually "ought to" be the slaves of the nation,
> could any philosopher be so unmanly, spiritless and weak, so resolved to
> make physical pleasure and pain the standard of everything, as to
> approve of this suggestion that the Senate is in bondage to the nation?[19]

But surely Crassus never thought the senate should be in bondage to
the nation. The truth is that the famous orator, seduced by the words
that would likeliest move his listeners, turned himself into an unthinking demagogue when he talked that way. It might be fairer to say that
a reflex assumption, almost inherent in the stock phraseology, trig-
gered the false attitude. Antonius himself had always assumed, on the
contrary, that the nation handed control to the senate as a passenger
in a horse-drawn coach gives the reins to the driver. Somewhere
under these criticisms of detail, however, may lurk the polemical
suggestion that the orator is by nature well acquainted with involuntary servitude. After all, he is a speaker whose livelihood depends on
his audience, and this requires the sort of wheedling for patronage and
votes that the dialectician (that is, the philosopher) has somehow
gotten free of.

If any defense is available to the orator, it must be related to his claim of a kind of civic courage; and this applies most of all to the forensic speaker, the virtuoso of courts and tribunals. Such orators are willing to be judged precisely by their partiality, and their effort to persuade comes from "our loyalty, sense of duty and carefulness [*fides, officium, diligentia*], under whose influence, even when defending complete strangers, we still cannot regard them as strangers, if we would be accounted good men ourselves."[20] This sense of the duty of justice to strangers is an ingrained principle of civic morale, and a principle likely to shoot forth in inspired moments of indignation that get the better of the speaker. The figure of speech that springs from such emotional exuberance is hyperbole, which shows the speaker feeling more than the occasion warrants. Or perhaps it shows that the occasion is different from what we took it to be.

* * *

The other side of justice to strangers is a sworn hostility to corruption and any abuse of privilege among ourselves. It was natural for Cicero's speeches against the corrupt Roman governor Verres to achieve a surprising penetration where they appeared at once hyperbolic and matter-of-fact: "Since Verres never let one minute go by without doing something wrong, I have simply been unable to acquaint myself with every villainy he has perpetrated."[21] We might sharpen the emphasis carried by the idea of persuasion if we took as the prototype of rhetorical action the prosecution or defense of an accused person in a public tribunal.

My examples in the next three lectures will favor a mood of sympathetic advocacy that occasionally verges on decision or final verdict. The artist of persuasive words must have been interested in such effects, since one must labor to acquire the ability to produce them; yet in the most rewarding instances, the achieved effect may have little to do with any deliberate aim. Words originally designed for a purpose can stir readers to feel a sensation (including or implying sympathy) that outruns the settled purpose of the words and that has no correlative in action.

And here, it seems, is a point of possible agreement among the ancient and modern rhetoricians, Aristotle, Cicero, Burke, and Austin. A reader always comes to particular words armed with an idea of what the words are likely to mean. But whereas the speaker in an everyday transaction says something in the *belief* that it will be interpreted in a certain way—and with the *expectation* that it will be so interpreted—the orator and the poet care for the impression conveyed as much as the understanding that is secured. If words overshoot their mark or diverge from the author's probable meaning, that is a risk of using words that carry a more than rational force. Nevertheless the words are understood; and the listener or interpreter is moved. One thinks (if at all) only later. The author has "gotten away with it," or the words have gotten away with the author.

2

Speakers Who Convince Themselves

Shakespeare, Milton, James

Persuasion commonly works by a semblance of reasoned argument in order to appeal directly and indirectly to the passions. Reason and passion are both necessary, of course, to the success of a speech that looks to reshape the will of its audience. Present the passions too harshly or vehemently and you won't clear a passage to admit a thought to the minds of listeners. On the other hand, supply only a well-ordered troop of reasons—however ably connected in logical form—and you will convert only people who live by reason and logic. And they are few. More important than reason, therefore, is the semblance of reason, which, as Aristotle pointed out in his *Rhetoric*, may include true or false logical sequences, well-attested evidence or specious evidence.

The drawn-out debate that may be said to occupy the first three acts of *Julius Caesar* turns on a series of ad hominem arguments that ask the question: Was Caesar a good man, and were his personal traits good for Rome? It depends on whether Caesar is the name of a benefactor who enriched the city or the name of an impending tyranny. Telling arguments are offered on both sides, and the conclusion we draw will follow from the way we judge the evidence inductively. The audience of the play is put in possession of the relevant facts and invited to judge; the words and actions that we witness can take us in either direction. Shall we emphasize Caesar's amiable dislike of fanaticism—his intuitive distrust of men like Cassius who have "a lean and hungry look" (because you cannot govern such people, and cannot easily govern *with* them)? Another possibly admirable quality is Caesar's tenderness, which produces a touch of pathos at the very moment of his death: *"Et tu, Brute?"* Still, one might as easily call

attention to his over-eager embrace of glory, his boastfulness—"I
rather tell thee what is to be feared / Than what I fear: for always
I am Caesar."[1] Do we come nearer the heart of the problem if we
notice the superstition that makes him dread the warnings of the
soothsayer? But again, that quality should be balanced against his
concern with appearances—a weakness in some settings, but one
that allows Caesar to overcome his fear as he confronts his accusers
in the Senate.

It is well to be reminded of the internal strangeness of the entire
process of persuasion; for convincing other people involves intentions
and tactics not essentially different from those we employ in convincing ourselves. Persuasion means the use of words to make others
believe something they were not disposed to believe, or anyway were
not disposed to agree with as strongly before we began to speak. By
what means do we bring them over? Among other methods, we call
upon their old and avowed beliefs. To say it another way, we show
that they already agree with themselves and that we agree with them
more than they think. Also, we try to exemplify belief in the stronger
form of conviction. The speaker is only surer than the audience of all
they thought was true; and so he deploys fresh facts, discoveries that
on their face testify for the side of the case he is pleading. Or he may
tell a story, but there, too, an appeal is made to psychological habit, to
conformity and continuity. The conclusion we want our listeners to
arrive at falls in with their already existing beliefs and shapes a
connected narrative of their interests over time.

What is sometimes said to be an elemental human "need for a
narrative" has been overrated by psychologists, literary theorists,
political handlers and spin doctors, and you will be hearing little
about it from me; but the hunger for belief *is* related to our common
love of stories, emphatically including true stories. Bertolt Brecht, one
of the few original theorists of the relationship between public performance and belief, advised actors to break up the deterministic
continuity of a play by seeming occasionally to stand outside their
roles. "It could have been this way and it also could have been that
way"—an actor's performance ought to be fertile in such suggestions in order to strengthen a dramatic therapy that treats the audience as thinking individuals, and not as a slack mass governed
by empathy and prepared for conversion. So Brecht wrote in his

"Short Description of a New Technique of Acting which Produces an Alienation Effect":

> When he appears on the stage, besides what he actually is doing he will at all essential points discover, specify, imply what he is not doing; that is to say he will act in such a way that the alternative emerges as clearly as possible, that his acting allows the other possibilities to be inferred and only represents one out of the possible variants. He will say for instance "You'll pay for that", and not say "I forgive you". [2]

The manner of transmitting forgiveness, that is to say, should somehow also imply the opposite of forgiveness. What Brecht is working against is the habitual process of logical elimination that pushes the story and the corresponding empathy along predictable lines and excludes alternative feelings, motives, actions, or moral shadings. "The technical term," he remarks, for this procedure of radical reform in the theater is "fixing the 'not ... but.'"

Persuasion, by its very nature, presses forward without a sidelong glance and has a blind investment in the exclusion of alternatives. It has no particular interest in even learning what was excluded, so long as it led to the right result. Brecht's hope was that by "fixing the 'not ... but'" one could disenchant the spell of persuasion that the theater traffics in as much as rhetoric does. All but one of the passages I will look at ends by succumbing to its own enchantment, but I wouldn't think it worthwhile to expound merely reckless and cynical arguments, efforts of persuasion that were meant to stampede the audience, set off a panic and compel surrender without any view of consequences. The examples that follow, on the contrary, seem to me interesting because they all incorporate a vivid semblance of thought.

* * *

Two likely fields of exercise lie open for an effort of persuasion. There is the speaker working to convince someone else, and there is the speaker convincing himself. Brutus in *Julius Caesar* is among the most instructive examples in drama of the second sort of address. He sees himself as someone who endures, more than someone who acts, and that is the way the part is usually played; but the dramatic action doesn't altogether bear out this view. It is not the republican zealot

Cassius but Brutus himself who initiates the dialogue in which Cassius will attempt to recruit him to the conspiracy:

> BRUTUS:
> What means this shouting? I do fear the people
> Choose Caesar for their king.
> CASSIUS: Ay, do you fear it?
> Then must I think you would not have it so.
>   (I.ii.79–81)

Brutus now confesses his dedication to honor, saying that the defense of his honor alone would be sufficient to move him to sacrifice himself, or to risk death in some daring enterprise. He thereby lays the psychological groundwork for the plot.

Brutus indeed, as he tells Cassius, loves honor more than he fears death; and this way of putting it gives a large clue to his character. The habit of balance and antithesis, turning morality into a series of topics for metaphysical reflection, somehow typifies the man: his strength and his weakness alike are visible here. Brutus is one who reflects and then acts. Cassius knows this and aims to use his knowledge. In order of composition, *Julius Caesar* came just before *Hamlet*, and there will be a good deal of Brutus in Hamlet; and yet Hamlet thinks more deeply, individually, spontaneously, suspects more and is more at the mercy of whim, with a nervous constant need of play and a mind that is apt to reduce his enterprises to nothing but play. Hamlet cannot back himself and plant his resolve on his instincts. Brutus can.

Cassius, in the harangue that follows about the want of stamina and physical courage in Caesar and the duty to resist a dictatorship that portends tyranny, is preparing to fashion Brutus to his own purpose, but he thinks he can do still more: "I your glass / Will modestly discover to yourself / That of yourself which you yet know not of." He makes of this venture at best a partial success; for both the intensely emotional and the oratorical elements in Cassius's speech are looking to exploit a resentment that hardly exists in Brutus. "Why, man, he doth bestride the narrow world / Like a colossus"—the trope is easy and available, and ought to take hold, but Brutus only hears the general shouts of the Roman crowd: they are what trouble him. Still, he catches the drift of the causerie against Caesar, in the other ear as it were, and gently chides Cassius for presuming on their friendship. They are formal and decent friends, no more than that:

> That you do love me, I am nothing jealous:
> What you would work me to, I have some aim:
> How I have thought of this and of these times
> I shall recount hereafter. For this present,
> I would not, so with love I might entreat you,
> Be any further moved.
>
> (I.ii.161–6)

Politely, he is instructing Cassius not to waste his breath; Brutus has already "thought of this" and it is *his* thoughts that will matter: the strenuous prepared address by Cassius has worked chiefly as a reminder. There are thoughts of his own, already acknowledged, that he would as soon have avoided, and Cassius has made them harder to avoid.

Beyond the republican and ad hominem reproaches against Caesar, two clear arguments are touched on by Cassius. He recalls the privileges and responsibilities that belong alike to Brutus and to himself as freemen; and he emphasizes the dignity of the idea of Roman fame. Since the two names Caesar and Brutus are equally weighty, why should they be differently valued? This is a public-spirited argument against tyranny, but it also favors the self-regarding motives that could drive any citizen to act so as to prevent tyranny. The two motives ought to be incompatible, or they can seem so anyway by our modern lights: high-minded equality on the one hand, among the representatives of civic virtue, and on the other hand aristocratic distinction. Yet both motives seem an intensification of an aspect of republican idealism that has been inculcated in Brutus and Cassius throughout their public lives. Brutus, then, listens to Cassius without being seduced, and it is important that we not take his listening as a surrender. We distrust Cassius more than Brutus does, and more than he needs to. We are apt to see Cassius as predatory, a hunter on the track of his quarry, but Brutus is not wrongly moved and is never at his mercy. He is the ascendant power in the friendship, as their scene of mutual reproach in Act IV will make plain.

* * *

We come now to Brutus in Act II, arguing the merits of the killing with a casuistic dryness. Casuistry, in the loosely pejorative sense, progresses from a desired conclusion to the arguments that most favor the conclusion, even as it goes through the motions of a sequential argument from honest premises. Brutus in his soliloquy will obey a more impartial method. He divides the case against Caesar into its different possible clues and inferences:

> It must be by his death: and for my part,
> I know no personal cause to spurn at him,
> But for the general. He would be crowned:
> How that might change his nature, there's the question.
> It is the bright day that brings forth the adder,
> And that craves wary walking. Crown him that,
> And then I grant we put a sting in him
> That at his will he may do danger with.
> Th'abuse of greatness is when it disjoins
> Remorse from power; and to speak truth of Caesar,
> I have not known when his affections swayed
> More than his reason. But 'tis a common proof,
> That lowliness is young ambition's ladder
> Whereto the climber upward turns his face;
> But when he once attains the upmost round
> He then unto the ladder turns his back,
> Looks in the clouds, scorning the base degrees
> By which he did ascend. So Caesar may.
> Then, lest he may, prevent. And, since the quarrel
> Will bear no colour for the thing he is,
> Fashion it thus: that what he is, augmented,
> Would run to these and these extremities.
> And therefore think him as a serpent's egg
> Which hatched, would as his kind grow mischievous,
> And kill him in the shell.
>
> (II.i.10–34)

Notice how Brutus says the word "and" where we would say "but"— "and for my part," "and to speak truth of Caesar." The disjunctive possibility is reviewed in his mind and marked for its probable value without any need of a grammatical stop. Even when alone, Brutus declines to admit the propriety of a merely personal and antagonistic motive. He questions the change that may come over Caesar only for the sake of "the general," the good of the republic and the opinion of the people. The people, after all, are by nature susceptible to flattery, and may yield to the demagogue an unsuspecting confidence in arguments for unchecked power.

Persons, like animals, often change their behavior according to climate and adaptation. To have achieved a new height of glory may bring forth something deadly in Caesar, just as the adder is brought out by the heat of the day. The metaphor looks less pedantic when one recognizes it is the sun that interests Brutus more than the snake: Rome would enter a different climate by giving extraordinary powers to this man; and once that is done, the man himself will surely change. The figure of the ladder seems far-fetched and stiff; lowliness *is* a ladder, though, if we think of the shoulders of the crowd hoisting up one man as their representative and then as their superior. He stoops to please them only to ingratiate himself with the powers they temporarily embody, but he thinks himself naturally a cloud-dweller, one of the gods.

All of these doubts in Brutus are provisional. They point to what *may* happen to Caesar once he is elevated. Even so, practical wisdom is bound to deal in probabilities; and in politics above all, fear of the worst takes precedence over hope for the best. "Then, lest he may, prevent." Brutus, in this moment, convinces himself that the assassination of Caesar is a necessary act, politically considered. But he wants very much to think that it is also right; and a fascinating turn in the speech occurs when he treats himself as a typical citizen who looks to be sure that his motive as well as his image is untarnished. "Fashion it thus" does not mean "Let's see if people can't be made to believe this." It means rather, "Let me think of it this way in order to see whether so grave an action may consist with the character of the good man I feel myself to be." This is a form of self-consoling therapy known to anyone who has felt driven to a course of conduct morally doubtful or ambiguous, but about which one is sure it is right and that no better possibility is open. To Brutus, the assassination of Caesar has become what William James in "The Will to Believe" would call a "genuine option," an option that is "forced, living, and momentous." Suppose that Caesar *is* the snake that he well may be. The danger then will grow larger with his power, so he must be crushed before the power matures. Again it is a question of probabilities. Murder on this reasoning could only be extenuated in politics, where criminal acts may eventually gain legitimacy through their success.

We began overhearing Brutus in mid-thought—"It must be by his death"—and the speech closes as it opened, with a careful figure of speech. The serpent's egg may seem an illicit metaphor, since Caesar (future) can hardly be the monstrous child of Caesar (past), unless he is already a monster, and that is more than we know. But in the logic of metaphor, which here tracks the logic of the passions, he is both the serpent and the egg. Ambition—power disjoined from remorse—makes men different from themselves, as a wicked child is different from his guiltless parents. Caesar is apt to turn into ambition's child.

Does this seem true of Caesar as we see him in the play? That is by no means clear. Yet the suspicion points to a thought about human nature which Shakespeare's other histories and tragedies bear out. Think of Hamlet's self-acquittal on arranging the killing of Rosencrantz and Guildenstern, "Why, man, they did make love to this employment. / They are not on my conscience," and the misgiving comment of Horatio: "Why, what a king is this!"—where the suggestion seems to be that Hamlet has set himself on the bloody path of kings whose means and ends of power he loathed. Think of Macbeth saying to Lady Macbeth, before he decides to kill Duncan, "I dare do all that may become a man; / Who dares do more, is none." We are always ready enough to excuse our actions, defend them, and frame a justification at any point before, during, and after the performance of the deed. Brutus is plotting ahead of his conscious reasoning. He is a perceptive analyst of motives, too, though he works from acquired learning and maxims, and without any apparent reliance on intuition.

Finally, Brutus in this soliloquy is also thinking back to his previous appearance on stage. It took place at the close of Act I, in his encounter with Caska and Cassius, where Caska, a witness to Antony and Caesar's incitement of the crowd, described the interaction with a telling emphasis on two details: the crown that was thrice offered to Caesar and thrice refused, and Caesar's attack of the falling sickness. These pictures have lodged in the mind of Brutus to incorporate, in a single thought, the frailty of the all-too-human Caesar and the palpable danger of Caesar once crowned as emperor.

The Brutus of Shakespeare has been poorly served by recent commentators, his talents too easily demoted in comparison with the demagogic brilliance shown by Antony in Act III. Admittedly, Brutus suffers when measured against a rhetorical genius who pulls out all the stops. Antony is a master of man's social nature, as a spellbinding orator ought to be; his virtuosity recalls that of his grandfather, Antonius, as Cicero portrays him in *De Oratore*. But to deprecate Brutus by this contrast is to miss a point central to Shakespeare's tragedy. Brutus knows what he is doing and what he is refraining from. He wouldn't make a speech like Antony's if he could, a speech whose purpose is to foment civil war. His eulogy over the body of Caesar looks to vindicate the conspiracy as a selfless act that will guide Rome once again into the paths of republican virtue. It is a passionate speech of its kind, but the fervor is directed toward ideals rather than persons, and it does not mention or try to summon popular passions and resentments. Normal politics grows out of Brutus's mode of address. Antony's speech, by contrast, is insurrectionary and can only serve an understanding that makes politics synonymous with the division between friend and enemy.

Let us say that Brutus's speech in Act III (which I will not be quoting in detail) translates for the crowd the very tactics he used to convince himself in Act II. These should be enough to persuade an intelligent citizen who is proud and slow to anger. And to whom else in the play could he defer? Cassius sets Brutus thinking, as the ghost will do for Hamlet; but thereafter, all the influential thoughts and motives belong to Brutus himself, and it is hard to see how they could be improved. We witness the stages of his reasoning, and we can see his process is partial and could mislead. None of this is visible from inside, nor would it be obvious to anyone else on the scene.

So Brutus in his soliloquy in Act II is self-serving, true enough, but he is also conscientious; and having convinced himself, he is prepared soon after to persuade Caius Ligarius: "Send him but hither and I'll fashion him." A curious phrase—so close to the words in the soliloquy itself—and, as Shakespeare must have thought, interestingly Roman. Once again, we may be tempted to think it means simply "I'll play on him"; but Brutus isn't boasting of his powers of manipulation. He can mean to fashion Caius Ligarius only in the same sense in which he has worked himself around, by a semblance of reasoned argument: "Fashion it thus." Indeed, one *ought* to be properly fashioned to the cause one serves, the better to adhere to that cause single-mindedly.

* * *

Pass now to Angelo in *Measure for Measure*: another character who listens to himself and makes of the work of judgment an intellectual discipline. "Save your honour,"[3] Isabella has said, bidding him goodbye till their appointed meeting; and as she departs, the first line of his soliloquy contains the germ of a complicated thought, which he accepts as a possible motive of action by speaking it. Save me, Angelo says,

> From thee: even from thy virtue!
> What's this? What's this? Is this her fault, or mine?
> The tempter, or the tempted, who sins most, ha?
> Not she; nor doth she tempt; but it is I
> That, lying by the violet in the sun,
> Do as the carrion does, not as the flower,
> Corrupt with virtuous season. Can it be
> That modesty may more betray our sense
> Than woman's lightness? Having waste ground enough,
> Shall we desire to raze the sanctuary
> And pitch our evils there? O, fie, fie, fie!
> What dost thou, or what art thou, Angelo?
> Dost thou desire her foully for those things
> That make her good? O, let her brother live!
> Thieves for their robbery have authority
> When judges steal themselves. What, do I love her,
> That I desire to hear her speak again?
> And feast upon her eyes? What is't I dream on?
> O cunning enemy, that, to catch a saint,
> With saints dost bait thy hook! Most dangerous
> Is that temptation that doth goad us on
> To sin in loving virtue. Never could the strumpet,
> With all her double vigour, art and nature,
> Once stir my temper: but this virtuous maid
> Subdues me quite. Ever till now,
> When men were fond, I smil'd, and wonder'd how.
>   (II.ii.162–87)

Character aside, there is a marked difference of moral stance between this soliloquy and the speech in which Brutus convinces himself. For Brutus has no doubt regarding his public stature and the need to mold his actions accordingly; his only question is about the moral character of Caesar—the change that has already occurred in Caesar or the change that will come over him. But he is so sure of himself that he can state the necessary deduction foremost—"It must be by his death"— then work back over the ground to prove that he is the proper executor of the result. Angelo presents almost an opposite instance. He has been shaken and made uncertain of who and what he is. His entire outlook crumbles when he recognizes that the incorruptible judge, too, is human, feels desire, and reveals imperfection already and demonstrably. Why may he not deviate in other respects as well? Angelo's subsequent reasoning with himself regards the terms of his contract with nature and justice: if such a thing, which should never happen, *can* happen, why may he not respond in ways that were never anticipated? If anything can happen, may not anything be permitted? The answer depends on the station of the observer: from outside, as a judge, not at all; from inside, as a desiring and dreaming person, an "I" who "am" in answer to the question "What art thou?"—from inside (if we can stay inside) the matter looks different. What is our humanity, once we free it from external judgment, if not a license for every transgression and (in the case of Angelo) an alibi for the necessary secrecy of a judge who takes his office seriously and means to retain it. The judge, as a single member of a society built on this morale, will be a hypocrite certainly, but no worse than other people, and the utilitarian case for his official standing remains strong: without someone acting as judge, transgression would become at once general *and shameless*. And it is not yet shameless, so long as the despoiled judge works out his corruptions in secret. The play has behind it a metaphysical supposition, namely that all justice depends on an anonymous inscrutable observer whose virtue is as much a mystery as the purity of commitment that binds a nun to her vows.

That observer is God or the Duke; and they may be much the same thing. Such justice as we have—both adequate and arbitrary—comes into the play through the selfless surveillance of the Duke in disguise. The faults of human nature seem to be ordered in such a way that someone must play this miraculous role. The perversely ingenious argument of Angelo's soliloquy confirms the allegory by its exposure of a merely human judge; the soliloquy is a credible specimen of an institutional conscience acquitting itself to itself. His recognition that, as a hypocrite, he may do more good than harm, and get away with it, actually hardens his determination to maintain an external show of faith in the presence of an inward knowledge of his weakness. Angelo closes the speech uneasy with himself, as he never expected to be, but sure of all that he thought was true.

What do we in the audience make of this? It is a series of bewildered questions uttered to himself by a man in torment; and that makes him at first an object of sympathy. We hear that Angelo prior to the interview has been stainless; and if the actor plays it delicately—without a glimmer of encouragement while Isabella is present—we will share his thrilled and mortified surprise at the record of his feelings. This is, in fact, the sort of inward experience that explains the exist-ence of the rite of confession—a variety of performative speech that requires, for its completion, the approval of its audience (the priest). But Angelo draws out the consciousness of his temptation with a coloring hardly available to a common mind: "Shall we desire to raze the sanctuary / And pitch our evils there?" We can imagine suffering such a fall; we know that we *have* suffered it, in imagination. And yet the constructive work of Angelo's soliloquy brings him all the way from temptation to surrender. He will act as both the fallible creature and the upright judge; and it is the necessity and fallibility of judgment that creates the human need for forgiveness. In this way, the soliloquy prepares us for the otherwise baffling happy ending of *Measure for Measure*. To the extent that we in the audience accept the ending, we have been helped by Angelo's spoken words of self-recognition.

* * *

Satan in Book I of *Paradise Lost* harbors no conception of himself as a judge or impartial observer of any kind whatever. He avows himself a creature of will, rather than laws, and he knows this from the start, from the inside out. This implies a distortion in his knowledge of external objects. His direction and purpose are never in doubt, yet Book I will show the degree of his uncertainty about how to accom-plish his aim, and his skill at concealing this from himself and others.

The opening speech contains thoughts that move faster than he can know. Its words are spoken in the service of convincing others, with an assurance for which he lacks adequate grounds himself. Satan, as he addresses Beelzebub, needs to console, to reason with, and to justify himself as well; but the obscurity of his situation renders his thoughts ambiguous, and the headlong momentum of the grammar buries his doubts under many hidden pauses, while he elaborates, questions, and finally turns on a double negative that can lead him forward again.

> If thou beest he; but O how fallen! how changed
> From him, who in the happy Realms of Light
> Clothed with transcendent brightness didst outshine
> Myriads though bright: if he whom mutual league,
> United thoughts and counsels, equal hope,
> And hazard in the glorious enterprise,
> Joined with me once, now misery hath joined
> In equal ruin: into what pit thou seest
> From what highth fallen, so much the stronger proved
> He with his thunder: and till then who knew
> The force of those dire arms? Yet not for those,
> Nor what the potent victor in his rage
> Can else inflict, do I repent or change,
> Though changed in outward lustre, that fixed mind
> And high disdain, from sense of injured merit,
> That with the mightiest raised me to contend,
> And to the fierce contention brought along
> Innumerable force of spirits armed
> That durst dislike his reign, and me preferring,
> His utmost power with adverse power opposed
> In dubious battle on the plains of heaven,
> And shook his throne. What though the field be lost?
> All is not lost; the unconquerable will,
> And study of revenge, immortal hate,
> And courage never to submit or yield:
> And what is else not to be overcome?
> That glory never shall his wrath or might
> Extort from me. To bow and sue for grace
> With suppliant knee, and deify his power,
> Who from the terror of this arm so late
> Doubted his empire, that were low indeed,
> That were an ignominy and shame beneath

> This downfall; since by fate the strength of gods
> And this empyreal substance cannot fail,
> Since through experience of this great event
> In arms not worse, in foresight much advanced,
> We may with more successful hope resolve
> To wage by force or guile eternal war
> Irreconcilable, to our grand foe,
> Who now triumphs, and in the excess of joy
> Sole reigning holds the tyranny of heaven.
>   (I.84–124)

"If thou beest he; but O how fallen"—Alastair Fowler says the broken grammar of the opening comes from Satan's lack of assurance that Beelzebub is even present before him.[4] This seems to me a true and vital observation. The speech implies uncertainty about whether the being who *is* present, and whom he knows himself to be addressing, is the same Beelzebub that he once knew—so much worse does he appear. He is hardly even a ruin of himself. But the element of doubt, I agree with Fowler, goes deeper. Satan is astonished in the oblivious pool, and, adapting himself to the strange element, is not sure how much to trust his memory or whether to credit what he thinks he sees. His speech to Beelzebub, through a mist of probable but fallible half-recognition, comes as close as we get to Satan's inward processes of thought until the soliloquy on Mount Niphates in Book IV.

At the same time, because Satan is an inveterate politician—a living carrier of persuasion, his verbal prowess geared to the response it looks for—he thinks of the shape in front of him (which may be his friend) as an audience to be brought over as quickly as possible. He goes to work at once, even as he begins to explore new thoughts in himself. Satan, then, is convincing himself along lines he may later adapt to convince others, and the result is a speech in which the logical jumps and transitions of perspective or point of view are as uncontrolled as the grammar at times is discontinuous. Yet we are hardly aware of this fact. The language gives out an unswerving assurance that he will prevail.

This seems a common feature of political discourse and the rhetoric of self-justification. We have all seen it and, when the view is not compelled, have stood at a sufficient distance to perceive what was happening; but no poet or dramatist ever traced the phenomenon with greater care than Milton in these lines. The plot of the speech (to call it that) brings Satan from a sure deliverance of the judgment that he should retreat to an irresistible pressure of belief that he must not surrender lest he cease to be himself, and finally to the resolution that the terms of his defeat and even his refusal of defeat are a proof that he may yet reverse his fate. Like some people one has known, he believes a thing as soon as he hears himself say it. He stands in possession of a new knowledge, or so he thinks, which if rightly used could bring him victory. On the way to a limited confession of weakness he picks up fresh signs of strength; they come in the shape of words that affirm the reality of actions that must follow words. Many speeches of concession after election defeats are something like this.

"And what is else not to be overcome?"—that is the critical phrase, and it is stirring beyond its susceptibility of translation into plain sense. Fowler gives two readings. First, *And the very idea of not being overcome— what else can it mean but this?* (a question that naturally rounds off the challenge). Second, *And whatever else it is in which not being overcome may consist* (a fragmentary noun clause rather than a completed question; in effect, the last item in a list; so that *and* becomes the important word and the rest says anything else you like).[5] I would add a third likely meaning: *And what more do you have to oppose against me, beyond everything I have seen and endured already?* ("It doesn't matter what the next obstruction is, I will keep overcoming whatever tries to overcome me, because I am indomitable"). Satan, on the last reading, is not to be overcome at any point. He persuades himself that his power is no less than it has always been; and not merely because he is not yet defeated. Rather he is himself still overcoming, still asking how anything can resist his will. ("What can there be in the visible or invisible world that I lack the ability to surmount? The more weight you load me with, the stronger I am.")

William Empson in *Milton's God* has a wonderful passage on the capability of Satan as a speaker during the war in heaven. He begins his speech in defiance of the declaration by God that he has delegated to his son "vicegerent" authority over all the angels:

> Thrones, dominations, princedoms, virtues, powers,
> If these magnific titles yet remain
> Not merely titular, since by decree
> Another now hath to himself engrossed
> All power, and us eclipsed under the name

> Of king anointed, for whom all this haste
> Of midnight march, and hurried meeting here,
> This only to consult how we may best
> With what may be devised of honours new
> Receive him coming to receive from us
> Knee-tribute yet unpaid, prostration vile,
> Too much to one, but double how endured,
> To one and to his image now proclaimed?
> But what if better counsels might erect
> Our minds and teach us to cast off this yoke?
> Will ye submit your necks, and choose to bend
> The supple knee? Ye will not, if I trust
> To know ye right, or if ye know your selves
> Natives and sons of heaven possessed before
> By none, and if not equal all, yet free,
> Equally free; for orders and degrees
> Jar not with liberty, but well consist.
> Who can in reason then or right assume
> Monarchy over such as live by right
> His equals, if in power and splendour less,
> In freedom equal?
>   (V.772–97)

Satan flatters the pride of the rebel angels by mention of the "magnific" titles they bear, and invites them to share his resentment at the naming of a new "king anointed," which if sustained would make a mockery of the titles. Besides, he adds, the new-named superior "hath to himself engrossed / All power"—this way of putting it is a figurative twisting of a figurative truth, but it opens the question whether God or his son is actually in command; whichever it may be, the power is absolute, and homage of "knee-tribute" was bad enough when paid to only one. The passage winds down with a further appeal to pride and self-worth: if the angels acquiesce in the humiliation and insult, they aren't possessed of the self-worth he assumed they shared as a virtue. Satan is nonetheless clear that they will recognize the truth he speaks in proportion as they know themselves. They are less than God only "in power and splendour"; in the republican practice of freedom, they are his equals.

T. S. Eliot had said that the speech showed Milton's want of invention, since Satan as we hear him is "not *thinking* or conversing, but making a speech carefully prepared for him, and the arrangement is for the sake of musical value, not for significance." Empson comments:

> It is odd to reflect that this was written while the spellbinder Lloyd George was still a power in the country. A speaker can at times feel so much in contact with the minds of a large audience that, instead of doing any of these three things [thinking, conversing, making a prepared speech], he invents at the moment what will swing them decisively on to his side; and here Satan is made to do it at the electric speed of thirty lines. It is so thrillingly "spoken" that one is driven to inquire why so good a critic could not understand how it was meant to be read.... The reason why Satan can win over his army so quickly is that they already hate God, or hate the recent ukase of God, so much that they do not require completed arguments; various points have to be cleared, but Satan can drop one sentence or argument and start another as soon as they are confident that he is taking the right line.[6]

This is almost enough to complete my thought on the opening speech of Book I. At work convincing himself, Satan exhibits the convergence of an instinct for improvisation—which tracks and assimilates the motives of his audience—and a restless desire to spread the nets of his own mind and prevent any doubt from escaping. He has no idea why he shifts ground like this, irritably and energetically, urging new questions and scattering them like seeds to sprout up arguments he can't catch a glimpse of. He drops one argument and takes up another as a matter not just of persuasion but almost of self-preservation. He does it to keep on being the self that he is. He does not realize that he is doing any of it. His verbal conduct embodies an extreme that proves the usual character of excited speech when it aims to convert a chosen audience.

* * *

Henry James's depiction of the stream of thought in Isabel Archer affords an internalized example of "convincing oneself" that is presented with the apparent detachment of third-person narrative. But here, the movement of mind is toward a knowledge which was always latent and true, but which required the language of analysis to be made true *for someone*. By a version of the free indirect style in narration, James extended the resources for portraying the act of convincing oneself; but the stakes are morally different here than in the soliloquies I quoted from Shakespeare and Milton. Isabel Archer's train of thought about her marriage is a kind of analysis that could lead to action under conditions of self-knowledge and sanity. In the plot of *The Portrait of a Lady*, however, her recognition has the nature of a dramatic reversal. It is a breaking-free that happens because of a real discovery of repressed knowledge. There is a sense in which she already knew all this and the discovery is an unforgetting.

Brutus, one might say, became aware of his responsibilities; Angelo saw a truth about his desire and his human composition; Satan came to know his changeless strength of mind and purpose; and in every case, these were recognitions the speakers could wrongly treat as revelations about the nature of things. Isabel, by contrast, deals with a world entirely constituted by ordinary human relations. Ideas such as patrician honor, the duty to resist tyranny, religious chastity, and judicial impartiality are not active in this world. There is more truth for her to find, but less inevitability in the finding.

She is persuading herself that she has already seen, already known, the circumstances that changed her fortune, but only now can she read the expression on the face and figure of those circumstances. I quote from Chapter 40:

> Just beyond the threshold of the drawing-room she stopped short, the reason for her doing so being that she had received an impression. The impression had, in strictness, nothing unprecedented; but she felt it as something new, and the soundlessness of her step gave her time to take in the scene before she interrupted it. Madame Merle was there in her bonnet, and Gilbert Osmond was talking to her; for a minute they were unaware she had come in. Isabel had often seen that before, certainly; but what she had not seen, or at least had not noticed, was that their colloquy had for the moment converted itself into a sort of familiar silence, from which she instantly perceived that her entrance would startle them. Madame Merle was standing on the rug, a little way from the fire; Osmond was in a deep chair, leaning back and looking at her. Her head was erect, as usual, but her eyes were bent on his. What struck Isabel first was that he was sitting while Madame Merle stood; there was an anomaly in this that arrested her. Then she perceived that they had arrived at a desultory pause in their exchange of ideas and were musing, face to face, with the freedom of old friends who

sometimes exchange ideas without uttering them. There was nothing to
shock in this; they were old friends in fact. But the thing made an
image, lasting only a moment, like a sudden flicker of light. Their
relative positions, their absorbed mutual gaze, struck her as something
detected. But it was all over by the time she had fairly seen it.[7]

And the process continues, along this path, the patient sifting of facts
understood and relations surmised, as Isabel interprets the signs made
accidentally available by her unintended glimpse of a partly familiar
scene. She does not deduce, from the relative positions of Osmond
and Madame Merle, "betrayal" or "adultery" or any other obvious
predicate; and in this she reveals a mind less bound by customary
perception than Brutus shows in his mental review of Caesar's posture
toward the Roman crowd, or Leontes in *The Winter's Tale* exclaiming
"Too hot, too hot" as he thinks over the scene he has witnessed
between Hermione and Polixenes. What Isabel recognizes is simply
that there has been a failure of candor between the pair of figures by
the fire and herself. The previous friendship of Osmond and Madame
Merle was a thing she had known of, but they hid from her its length
and character. And the fact of this concealment may somehow implicate her freedom.

"It is fair to say," wrote George Herbert Mead in 1913, "that the
modern western world has lately done much of its thinking in the form
of the novel"; for the novel supplied "that need of filling out the bare
spokesman of abstract thought, which even the most abstruse thinker
feels."[8] Thought is a different thing from personality, Mead suggests;
but in the conditions of modern society, thought has needed to inhabit
a personality in order to penetrate our understanding. Otherwise we
are left with the bareness of "abstract thought" without a carrier of its
effects. Speech (if I catch the drift of Mead's sentence) mediates
between thought and the effects of thought; novels demonstrate this
relation for us as the characters come to know one another. Iris
Murdoch took this discovery to define the peculiar greatness of
nineteenth-century realism: "We may be tempted to forget how
almost impossibly difficult it is to create a free and lifelike character.
Or to feel that this particular effort is worth making."[9] The largest
significance of the effort must lie in the cooperation it shows between
knowledge of others and self-knowledge.

The meditation by Isabel Archer finds its proper conclusion two chapters later, with her disenchanted recognition of what her marriage to Osmond has been:

> A gulf had opened between them over which they looked at each other with eyes that were on either side a declaration of the deception suffered. It was a strange opposition, of the like of which she had never dreamed—an opposition in which the vital principle of the one was a thing of contempt to the other. . . . It was her deep distrust of her husband—this was what darkened the world. That is a sentiment easily indicated, but not so easily explained, and so composite in its character that much time and still more suffering had been needed to bring it to its actual perfection. Suffering, with Isabel, was an active condition; it was not a chill, a stupor, a despair; it was a passion of thought, of speculation, of response to every pressure. She flattered herself that she had kept her failing faith to herself, however,—that no one suspected it but Osmond. Oh, he knew it, and there were times when she thought he enjoyed it.[10]

The sustained analysis of her predicament reaches its climax in the sentence: "They were strangely married, at all events, and it was a horrible life."

James there gives a summary of a settled condition; and he may seem to describe a condition of unfreedom. Yet, by the very energy of the self-examination, the footsteps of thinking traced by the protagonist and interpreted by the author, we have been made to know this not merely as a scene of mental suffering. It is "an active condition," "a passion of thought"—James is willing to risk even those phrases which border on insistence, to convey the reality of the self-command Isabel has come to know unmistakably. Chapter 42 shows the end of her passage from intimation to persuasion to conviction. It is, of course, only a possibility that this recognition will lead to a different life: a life she could know as her own—an emergence from her particular past—and yet a life she would not think of calling "horrible." If that seems a tentative conclusion, it suits the temperament of Henry James, who, as much as his brother, was interested in the question "What may the word 'possible' definitely mean?"[11]

I suspect that James heeded the examples of Shakespeare and Milton to learn what he was aiming at in the dialogue of Isabel Archer with herself. He had other available sources, no doubt, among the nineteenth-century novelists; a major forerunner is certainly the all-night meditation that leads Dorothea Brooke, in *Middlemarch*, to an inward recognition of the truth about her marriage. But James is interested in an account of consciousness that seeks no effect. Not to sway us to the side of a favored character, not even for a moment. And not to let us think for her: "Now this is what you must do."

From the compositional details of these two central passages, one may derive a defense of Isabel's choice at the end of the novel (bewildering on the face of it) to reject the love of Casper Goodwood, the chivalrous suitor to whom she is powerfully drawn. The defense comes from the perception of heroism in the very withdrawal from productive action—a kind of heroism described in the commentaries on Austen and Hardy by Anne-Lise François in *Open Secrets*. Chapters 40 and 42 of *The Portrait of a Lady* bear witness to a return from action to thought that is also an achievement of freedom.

Words are constantly interpreted. That is a usual way that they register an effect—whether or not we can say for sure that they have been rightly understood. For words to defy interpretation and understanding and to remain opaque, obscure, blank, unmeaning, or somehow suspended before an uncertain intelligence—such a privation, if we could imagine it, would eliminate every effect and would lead to despair instead of understanding, and renunciation instead of action. Henry James, I believe, was on the trail of something different from either of those results. His deepest interest lies in the impression conveyed rather than the understanding secured or the action that follows the understanding. His method asks a question. Can we imagine a language appropriate to a perceptive mind that sees and tells the truth about people without wanting to have any power over them? Mastery of such a language would begin with a vow of separation between knowing and doing. And Isabel at the end of the novel is not far from such a vow. A world of pure experience, if we could imagine it, would be a world in which the devices of persuasion dissolve in the sheer activity of thought and feeling. The wished-for result could never be simply to settle a disputation; but we always knew there were other things to wish for. Conclusion and conversion do not signify the attainment of truth.

3

Pledging Emotion for Conviction

Burke, Lincoln, Bagehot

Persuasion requires that we have feelings about beliefs. We feel we ought to sympathize with other people, for example, and we have brought into usage an arcane word, "empathy," to prove how thoroughly we are impressed by the sympathetic imperative. Empathy means feeling *as* the other person, feeling as if inside him or her, not just feeling *with* or feeling *for*. How much of this goes on? Less than we say, perhaps; but there were reasons for thinking that sympathy, as commonly understood, was too weak an idea to imply the quasi-moral imperative we wanted to attach to such a feeling. A word was needed to suggest emotions that implicate duties, feelings that show with ostensive immediacy that we are in the presence of a human trouble which requires attention and action. There are plenty of expressions that do cover this ground: *please attend to this closely* (we say), *this deserves your attention*—which may well mean that someone deserves your help. Still, why was ordinary sympathy thought to be not enough?

A familiar passage from Adam Smith's *Theory of Moral Sentiments* brings out the nature of the problem. Sympathy, according to Smith, either impinges on me or it doesn't. If it does, the reason lies in a resemblance I can feel (in an uncomplicated perceptual way) with the person and predicament I am confronted by. The person and predicament remind me of something about myself or my own predicament; I suppose that if I fail to act here with a modicum of generosity and consideration, I as much as ask to be treated inadequately when I am found in the same situation. There is thus an implied reciprocity in the act of sympathy which induces a reasonable fear of retribution or comeuppance from the neglect of sympathy. At least, we can suppose it does so, if moral causes and effects in society work in as orderly a manner as the system of heaven and hell. If an analogy is wanted, think of the way a failure of self-respect may bring a loss of respect from others.

Here is the relevant passage from Smith:

> Let us suppose that the great empire of China, with all its myriads of inhabitants, was suddenly swallowed up by an earthquake, and let us consider how a man of humanity in Europe, who had no sort of connexion with that part of the world, would be affected upon receiving intelligence of this dreadful calamity. He would, I imagine, first of all, express very strongly his sorrow for the misfortune of that unhappy people, he would make many melancholy reflections upon the precariousness of human life, and the vanity of all the labours of man, which could thus be annihilated in a moment. He would too, perhaps, if he was a man of speculation, enter into many reasonings concerning the effects which this disaster might produce upon the commerce of Europe, and the trade and business of the world in general. And when all this fine philosophy was over, when all these humane sentiments had been once fairly expressed, he would pursue his business or his pleasure, take his repose or his diversion, with the same ease and tranquillity, as if no such accident had happened. The most frivolous disaster which could befal himself would occasion a more real disturbance. If he was to lose his little finger to-morrow, he would not sleep to-night; but, provided he never saw them, he will snore with the most profound security over the ruin of a hundred millions of his brethren, and the destruction of that immense multitude seems plainly an object less interesting to him, than this paltry misfortune of his own. To prevent, therefore, this paltry misfortune to himself, would a man of humanity be willing to sacrifice the lives of a hundred millions of his brethren, provided he had never seen them? Human nature startles with horror at the thought, and the world, in its greatest depravity and corruption, never produced such a villain as could be capable of entertaining it. But what makes this difference? When our passive feelings are almost always so sordid and so selfish, how comes it that our active principles should often be so generous and so noble? When we are always so much more deeply affected by whatever concerns ourselves, than by whatever concerns other men; what is it which prompts the generous, upon all occasions, and the mean upon many, to sacrifice their own interests to the greater interests of others? It is not the soft power of humanity, it is not that feeble spark of benevolence which Nature has lighted up in the human heart, that is thus capable of counteracting the

strongest impulses of self-love. It is a stronger power, a more forcible
motive, which exerts itself upon such occasions. It is reason, principle,
conscience, the inhabitant of the breast, the man within, the great judge
and arbiter of our conduct. It is he who, whenever we are about to act
so as to affect the happiness of others, calls to us, with a voice capable of
astonishing the most presumptuous of our passions, that we are but one
of the multitude, in no respect better than any other in it; and that when
we prefer ourselves so shamefully and so blindly to others, we become the
proper objects of resentment, abhorrence, and execration. . . . It is not the
love of our neighbour, it is not the love of mankind, which upon many
occasions prompts us to the practice of those divine virtues [of generosity,
self-sacrifice, and active benevolence]. It is a stronger love, a more
powerful affection, which generally takes place upon such occasions;
the love of what is honourable and noble, of the grandeur, and dignity,
and superiority of our own characters.[1]

The passage aims at a comprehensive explanation of the motives for
unselfish action, and if we grant the adequacy of Smith's idiom, which
turns on belief in the reciprocal workings of the interests and the
affections, his explanation covers the necessary ground. But one
thing we were looking to gain from sympathy was a way of overcoming our distance from—the temptation to be indifferent to—persons
and predicaments that ought to concern us. Smith, as appears from
his conspectus of the relevant duties and his analysis of the action of
sympathy in the passage above, cannot help us here. He writes with
civilized regret about the detachment felt by "a man of humanity . . .
upon receiving intelligence" of a catastrophe that occurs elsewhere to
persons remote from his position. This habitual license of disregard
makes it possible for me to feel in no way implicated in the far-off
deaths of millions of people, and to feel less pity for them than I do for
myself at the loss of a finger. What saves our self-love from ultimate
reproach, what Smith would like us to think may atone for the absence
of remorse by a mitigation of selfishness, is not a desire to expiate our
original indifference and reform our feelings—the sort of counteraction of feeling that Wordsworth a generation later hoped to induce
in readers of *Lyrical Ballads*. Instead, by way of remedy Smith offers to
filter the mood of indifference through an internal mechanism of
third-person oversight. This device to assist a therapy of self-induced
shame he calls "the inhabitant of the breast," the "impartial spectator"

or supervisory agent within, which rouses us from the indolence of self-regard and plants a wish to perform actions corresponding to the intense feeling one ought to have. Love, or intensely felt compassion, has only a supporting role in this mechanism, according to Smith. I improve myself from a desire to be seen as someone who might be called honorable or noble, someone whose actions might be felt to have a certain dignity. I wish to be seen by myself as a person of this sort—I am indeed seeing myself as others might see me, in order to become the sort of person I would like others to think I am.

* * *

The work of reflective feelings, as Adam Smith has described them, follows a pattern suggested by David Hume's account of pride. I am proud of a possession or an attribute because another person would have reason to be proud of such things and I can see myself as that other person. For example: I am proud of my house in large measure because I can see it as a visitor would, and I can think, with a visitor's sensibility, "That is an elegant house; it says something about its owner; he is entitled to some pride in it." Thus, feelings can often perform the work of understanding, as Donald Davidson showed in his essay "Hume's Cognitive Theory of Pride." The impressive passage from Smith's *Moral Sentiments* traces a similar circular psychology. It makes a satisfactory directive that may turn a child (with the lawless freedom of childhood) into someone who knows how to behave properly in society; someone who knows, also, how to behave when out of the view of significant members of his usual conforming group. Smith's psychology falls short, however, when we apply it for the purpose he intended and treat it as an account of the workings of sympathy. It omits, and seems perhaps unaware of, complexities that poetry and fiction of the following age would account for by an agency as mysterious as Smith's "man within," namely the workings of the human heart.

Burke included a section on sympathy in his *Enquiry into the Sublime and Beautiful*, the expanded edition of which appeared the same year as the *Theory of Moral Sentiments*. His definition is concise and almost casual, beside Smith's, but precisely for its lack of elaboration it does better justice to the emotion in its simplest form. Burke calls sympathy "a sort of substitution by which we are put into the place of another

man, and affected in many respects as he is affected." This sounds
close to Rousseau's description of pity in the *Discourse on Inequality*,
though Burke's definition is more parsimonious. The cry of nature, for
Rousseau, strikes our ear, we cannot choose but listen, and having
heard, we explore, participate, and somehow respond to an impulse to
help the sufferer. In the discussions of political speeches that follow,
I would like to keep in mind both Smith's prudential third-person
characterization of sympathy and the Romantic second-person understanding shared by Rousseau and Burke.

The most difficult task in politics—the reason for something called
statesmanship to exist—is to awaken public sentiments against an
entrenched abuse and convince lawmakers and public opinion to act
for the improvement of justice. Success in this area is hard to measure,
but one index of success in persuasion is a change of government.
Burke, in his *Speech at Bristol Previous to the Election* of 1780, confessed to
sentiments regarding the American colonists and English Catholics
that might have appeared sufficiently strange to cost him the Bristol
constituency; yet he was striking the chord of a possible sympathy,
which he believed might find an echo in his audience. His point of
entry on Catholic rights was the recent passage of Sir George Savile's
Act for the relief of Catholics from certain penalties and disabilities—a
liberal reform that Burke supported, and that had done much to
provoke the Gordon Riots three months earlier. Burke, however,
was impenitent:

> I confess to you freely, that the sufferings and distresses of the people of
> America in this cruel war, have at times affected me more deeply than
> I can express. I felt every Gazette of triumph as a blow upon my heart,
> which has an hundred times sunk and fainted within me at all the
> mischiefs brought upon those who bear the whole brunt of war in the
> heart of their country. Yet the Americans are utter strangers to me; a
> nation, among whom I am not sure, that I have a single acquaintance.
> Was I to suffer my mind to be so unaccountably warped; was I to keep
> such iniquitous weights and measures of temper and of reason, as to
> sympathize with those who are in open rebellion against an authority
> which I respect, at war with a country which by every title ought to be,
> and is most dear to me; and yet to have no feeling at all for the
> hardships and indignities suffered by men, who, by their very vicinity,
> are bound up in a nearer relation to us; who contribute their share, and

more than their share, to the common prosperity; who perform the
common offices of social life, and who obey the laws to the full as well as
I do? Gentlemen, the danger to the state being out of the question (of
which, let me tell you, statesmen themselves are apt to have but too
exquisite a sense) I could assign no one reason of justice, policy, or
feeling, for not concurring most cordially, as most cordially I did
concur, in softening some part of that shameful servitude, under
which several of my worthy fellow-citizens were groaning.[2]

Two sorts of distance are evoked here and compared for what they
may say about the motives of justifiable action derived from sympathy. The Americans are "like us"; more particularly, they are like
the Dissenters in Bristol whose votes Burke needed in 1780 and
whose interests he felt obligated to serve. The first sort of distance,
then, can be counted in miles. Bristol is closer than Boston; some of
our neighbors are being killed by Americans, and that makes fellow-
feeling with the colonists harder. By contrast, in the case of English
Catholics we have to cross a distance of manners only, of habits and
practices that reflect religious beliefs. The English Catholics are
neighbors in a more conspicuous and daily sense: sympathy with
them for the injustices of the law should not present a greater
difficulty than sympathy with the Americans for the injuries they
suffer in the war. This is an argument of the *a fortiori* kind: once the
humanity of concern for Americans is admitted—however extreme
the manifestation of it by a passionate member of the opposition
like Burke—so much the more allowable must be his feeling for
Catholics and his support of the legal measure that carried that
feeling into action.

* * *

Reform of the government of British India required a different pressure of conviction. Here, there was no such substantial loss of life
among people who could easily remind English people of themselves.
The loss of funds, on the other hand, was already known to the House
of Commons, whose members had not protested the subsidizing by
the East India Company of surrogate landlords and proxy warriors.
Yet two years after the defeat of Fox's East India Bill in 1783, Burke in
his speech on Almas Ali Khan signaled his determination to continue
his exposure of the corruption of the Company. He would pass now

beyond the Select Committee reports to the laborious work of accusation and impeachment.

Almas Ali Khan was a farmer and a collector of revenue for the company, from whom (as Burke describes the transaction) the governor-general, Warren Hastings, first extorted contributions before trying to have him killed. A third-person report of the speech was given in the *Parliamentary Register*:

> The contest was now reduced to a few simple facts, which the meanest understanding could comprehend as well as the most accomplished. [And laying his hand on a volume of the Reports which lay on the table] I swear, said he, by this book, that the wrongs done to humanity in the eastern world, shall be avenged on those who have inflicted them: They will find, when the measure of their iniquity is full, that Providence was not asleep. The wrath of Heaven would sooner or later fall upon a nation, that suffers, with impunity, its rulers thus to oppress the weak and innocent. We had already lost one empire, perhaps, as a punishment for the cruelties authorised in another. And men might exert their ingenuities in qualifying facts as they pleased, but there was only one standard by which the Judge of all the earth would try them. It was not whether the interest of the East-India Company made them necessary, but whether they coincided with the prior interests of humanity, of substantial justice, with those rights which were *paramount to all others*.[3]

The reference to the prior interests of humanity—and Burke does mean that these interests have moral priority over the political and economic self-interest of Britain—is most unusual in writings on international justice before Kant.

Beyond the claim of human nature as an aggregate entity (attention to which carries with it certain imperatives of action), the words I have just quoted are striking for their appeal to a power of retribution within the moral order. The wicked actions countenanced by a nation must be charged against the nation itself that permits the injustice. Nor will the retribution cease with the punishment of the few who can be named and accurately condemned as efficient causes of the evil. As it fell out, Burke's decision to impeach Hastings meant that the justice of his cause would be impaired by the choice of a single symbolic culprit. And yet the defection of Parliament from its normative duties of oversight had left him little choice. "Impeachment," as Richard

Bourke sums up, "would be Burke's instrument of representation;"[4] and this in a setting where—for the governed in India as well as the government in England—representation had been nullified.

In the trial of Hastings by the House of Commons before the House of Lords, Burke concentrated his accusations against the species of power Hastings had wrongly arrogated to himself. But the real premise of Burke's argument is that the corrupt governor stands for the system of unchecked power and patronage that supported him. The system in India had been perpetuated by extortionate threats of the total withdrawal of livelihoods from persons whose only offense was that they had money to give. Burke uses an old name to characterize the presumption that Hastings had incorporated in his procedures: it was a system of *arbitrary power*. Hastings justified it by claiming that deference to such power was habitual among the natives of India since it was a usual expedient of their conquerors.

Burke responded directly to this line of defense:

> Nothing is more false than that despotism is the constitution of any country in Asia that we are acquainted with. It is certainly not true of any Mahomedan constitution. But if it were, do your Lordships really think that the nation would bear, that any human creature would bear, to hear an English governor defend himself on such principles. . . .
>
> *He* have arbitrary power! My Lords, the East India Company have not arbitrary power to give him; your Lordships have not; nor the Commons, nor the whole legislature. We have no arbitrary power to give, because arbitrary power is a thing which neither any man can hold nor any man can give. No man can lawfully govern himself according to his own will; much less can one person be governed by the will of another. We are all born in subjection,—all born equally, high and low, governors and governed, in subjection to one great, immutable, pre-existent law, prior to all our devices and prior to all our contrivances, paramount to all our ideas and all our sensations, antecedent to our very existence, by which we are knit and connected in the eternal frame of the universe, out of which we cannot stir. . . .
>
> The title of conquest makes no difference at all. No conquest can give such a right; for conquest, that is, force, cannot convert its own injustice into a just title, by which it may rule others at its pleasure. . . .
>
> No, my Lords, this arbitrary power is not to be had by conquest. Nor can any sovereign have it by succession; for no man can succeed to fraud, rapine, and violence. Neither by compact, covenant, or

submission,—for men cannot covenant themselves out of their rights and their duties—nor by any other means, can arbitrary power be conveyed to any man. . . .

Law and arbitrary power are in eternal enmity. Name me a magistrate, and I will name property; name me power, and I will name protection. It is a contradiction in terms, it is blasphemy in religion, it is wickedness in politics, to say that any man can have arbitrary power. In every patent of office the duty is included. For what else does a magistrate exist? To suppose for power is an absurdity in idea. Judges are guided and governed by the eternal laws of justice, to which we are all subject. We may bite our chains, if we will, but we shall be made to know ourselves, and be taught that man is born to be governed by law; and that he that will substitute *will* in the place of it is an enemy of GOD.[5]

The English are a law-abiding people: that is the tacit knowledge that impels Burke's decomposition of the idea of arbitrary power.

Nor should his listeners bear to think otherwise. "An Englishman is the unfittest person in the world to argue another Englishman into slavery"—so Burke had said in the American context in 1775. The related argument here depends on a connection between manners and the delivery of substantial justice to strangers. Included in the understanding of manners, however, is the content of the public sentiments we avow concerning such principles as limited government and self-restraint. Pride is an element of such public feelings. If pride has not normally been supposed a tributary of justice, this only shows that in many respects our analysis of the motives of action has been unimaginative. Parliament and the people who permitted the abuses of the Company are now asked to acknowledge the shame of having countenanced an unjust exercise of power over strangers. Burke is saying that we ought to be too proud act as masters, just as we are too proud to submit as slaves.

To take to oneself the privilege of domination requires a denial of the restraint imposed on us by the social nature that we obey among neighbors and fellow citizens. Our fetters will only bind us tighter from the refusal to admit that we live under a previous and necessary subordination to natural law. The conduct of a restrained liberty, Burke believes, has become second nature to the British, but they will lose it for themselves if they deny it to the people whom they ought to govern generously. There is a historical component in this argument, and though it occupies a lower moral ground, it may form the toughest layer of Burke's appeal to sentiment. The British are a people of the covenant—a political covenant going back to the Great Charter. You cannot, in an agreement between equals, yourself consent to become a slave; you have discountenanced mastery in every arbitrary shape; and by the same measure, no one acting in correspondence with you can justly violate the understanding that backs the historical pledge. There is, however, another feature of Burke's argument, less available to us now but explicit in the phrasing of his *Speech on Fox's East India Bill* in 1783 and implicit in his conduct of the Hastings trial starting in 1788. The British Empire is felt to represent "the natural equality of mankind at large." Its servants therefore cannot rightly govern as if there were a natural inequality between the races of humankind, or as if accidental inequalities were themselves a crime. In this sense, Burke's argument for accountability in India, and his argument against a spirit of leveling and uniformity in the enactments of the French Revolution, are in complete accord. That revolution, as Burke saw it, was from the first a war against property, against prejudice, against religion, and against all the means by which human beings learn to restrain the operation of greed and envy that can overturn a whole society.

* * *

Burke's earlier speeches concerning India have on the whole made better sense to modern readers than his several-day-long orations in the trial of Hastings, with their dramatic emphasis, their drawn-out interrogations of evidence, and their reiterative technique. Yet the latter setting, I think, reveals more about the originality of his genius in the work of persuasion. As a prosecutor, Burke could deploy a rhetoric that was not minutely tactical. He thought the abuse in question, whereby the demand for company profits took priority over the interests of the people of India, was so likely to continue if unreproved—and the implications for the fate of the empire were so distressing—that only a recovered understanding of English liberty could justify the British remaining where they had been placed by "the Sovereign Disposer."[6] Only a radical revision of laws and policy would enable the governors of a distant and wrongly subordinated people to "do the best we can in our situation." His stubborn and taxing awareness of the challenge may in part account for the wildness of his words over many stretches of the parliamentary impeachment: a trait observed by all, and initially allowed for, but increasingly wondered at even by Burke's own party, and finally seized upon as grounds to discredit both the trial and Burke himself. He was hoping to create what did not yet exist at a level commensurate with a revolutionary age, namely an emotion of conviction with which the British people could recognize the extent of their responsibilities as citizens of an empire.

For assistance in describing the nature of the task that confronted Burke, let us turn to Walter Bagehot's remarkable essay "On the Emotion of Conviction." Clearness, intensity, constancy, and interestingness are the qualities, according to Bagehot, by which the presence of conviction may be known. Conviction thus shows itself to be a state of mind and feeling as involuntary as a passion:

> A hot flash seems to burn across the brain. Men in these intense states of mind have altered all history, changed for better or worse the creed of myriads, and desolated or redeemed provinces and ages. Nor is this intensity a sign of truth, for it is precisely strongest in those points in which men differ most from each other.[7]

The credulity we observe in children is also related to conviction, for children, says Bagehot, believe everything a grown-up says to them.

He contrasts this instant receptivity with what it means to be won over gradually by an argument that makes sense and offers evidence. Could a rational argument take hold so intensely as to exert a comparable influence? Could it draw credence from a train of connected reasons and at the same time command the power of untutored feelings? "Dry minds," remarks Bagehot,

> which give an intellectual "assent" to conclusions, which feel no strong glow of faith in them, often do not know what their opinions are. They have every day to go over the arguments again, or to refer to a notebook to know what they believe. But intense convictions make a memory for themselves, and if they can be kept to the truths of which there is good evidence, they give a readiness of intellect, a confidence in action, a consistency in character, which are not to be had without them.[8]

The conviction Bagehot is describing sounds as if it were essentially religious. But one can't deny the possibility that education, the conscious cultivation of sentiments with a non-religious object, could produce a state of mind just as unshakable. Bagehot remarked elsewhere that Burke "had the passions of more ordinary men in a degree, and of an intensity, which ordinary men may be most thankful that they have not." The preceding quotations from Burke's speeches have aimed to show how the emotion of conviction may inhabit a consecutive argument and function there as a proof of passion. But the examples have a more general significance. In an otherwise intelligent and reliable speaker, sincerity at this pitch will be taken as an indication of truth. The speaker avows that his connection with his cause is not a matter of convenience or expedient compromise; that it comes from a profound commitment and will persist undeterred by failures that might discourage an average partisan. One possible effect may be to spur in listeners a corresponding intensity of feeling.

* * *

F. H. Bradley published "My Station and its Duties" as a chapter of his book *Ethical Studies* in 1876, five years after Bagehot's essay; and Bradley there demoted conscience (or conviction of the sudden-revelatory kind) as a possible basis for moral judgment and action. Yet Bradley does speak of the mind of the community in terms strikingly suggestive of the "hot flash" that shows clearness, intensity, and interestingness all at once, and that proves its depth by its constancy:

> The soul [in the believer who knows his duties], is saturated, is filled, is qualified by, it has assimilated, has got its substance, has built itself up from, it *is* one and the same life with the universal life, and if he turns against this he turns against himself; if he thrusts it from him, he tears his own vitals; if he attacks it, he sets his weapon against his own heart. He has found his life in the life of the whole, he lives that in himself.[9]

The whole that Bradley has in view, it should be said, is the imputed organic life of a nation, a community so entirely established that it can evoke unconscious identification. England was like that for Bradley, and he took the title of his essay from the catechism in the Book of Common Prayer. Would it be possible to evoke such strength of

conviction on behalf of a creed and a community not yet supported by
a deep past?

That was the question that Abraham Lincoln put to himself and
spoke aloud when in the mid-1850s he began to argue against the
extension of slavery. Lincoln could not have cherished anything like
Burke's assurance about the customs and habits that instruct us in our
duties toward neighbors and strangers. But it may be fairer to say that
this sort of inheritance in the United States was bound to be political,
not religious—as can be seen from Lincoln's earlier wish for a "political religion" that commits Americans merely to abide by existing
laws. The entrenched abuse he sought to reform, however, had
already endured for more than two centuries. The power of the
slave-holding interest prevented any such intuitive opening for reform
as Burke thought he could perceive in 1788 for an oppression that
began in 1757.

Yet Lincoln aspired far more steadily than Burke to convince his
audience of the natural equality of mankind at large. He thought his
strongest help could come from the recollection of a single idea, an
abstract principle which had familiar correlatives in the daily experience of democracy. The principle was explained by the phrase "All
men are created equal." Lincoln chose to emphasize rather than
soften its abstractness by often calling it a "proposition"; and for
eleven years, starting in 1854, when expounding his political beliefs
he was always definitive and contentious on this point.

The arguments Lincoln advanced against slavery in the 1850s
resemble Burke's on the reform of India, in that they draw large
inferences from the way citizens ought to acknowledge the humanity
of persons they rule. We generally do this, Lincoln notices, even as we
continue to oppress them. Thus, in a public letter of 1863, in the
middle of the Civil War, he will adduce the Lockean argument that
personal rights apply to conscious persons who can keep promises.
Negroes are promise-keeping persons, as much as white people; a
promise has been made to them, of freedom in return for service in the
Union army; and "the promise being made, must be kept." If, that is,
former slaves fight to preserve the Union, on the understanding that
in doing so they become fellows of the freemen at whose side they
risk their lives, all citizens are obliged to admit the justice of
emancipation.

Lincoln had explored this argument nine years earlier in a more tentative way, at the end of his Speech on the Kansas-Nebraska Act of 1854:

> [Senator and formerly Judge Stephen Douglas has just told us], in substance, that he had always considered this government was made for the white people and not for the negroes. Why, in point of mere fact, I think so too. But in this remark of the Judge, there is a significance, which I think is the key to the great mistake (if there is any such mistake) which he has made in this Nebraska measure. It shows that the Judge has no very vivid impression that the negro is a human; and consequently has no idea that there can be any moral question in legislating about him. In his view, the question of whether a new country shall be slave or free, is a matter of as utter indifference, as it is whether his neighbor shall plant his farm with tobacco, or stock it with horned cattle. Now, whether this view is right or wrong, it is very certain that the great mass of mankind take a totally different view. They consider slavery a great moral wrong; and their feeling against it, is not evanescent, but eternal. It lies at the very foundation of their sense of justice; and it cannot be trifled with. It is a great and durable element of popular action, and, I think, no statesman can safely disregard it.[10]

Again here, as with Burke on Catholic disabilities, we have the intuition of a universal feeling which we may try to hide from ourselves, but which daily practice constantly brings to light.

Many Americans believe that the Negro is a human being and at the same time agree to live in a country where Negroes are treated as commodities like any other. And—what is natural but also strange— they act as decent neighbors toward persons who perpetuate that mode of treatment. Lincoln will emphasize in other speeches that we ourselves, even we of the North, perpetuate that treatment when we agree not to say and therefore (so far as we can put our thoughts into line with our habits) not to *think* that slavery is wrong. We deny for the sake of expedience what we know by sympathy, namely the "monstrous injustice" of slavery itself.

Lincoln's opponent Stephen Douglas, in the Illinois senate contest of 1858, with his doctrine of "popular sovereignty" which allowed a majority to decide as they pleased for or against slavery in the new territories, always spoke of slavery with a disciplined detachment.

Douglas was a racist, as Lincoln was not, but Douglas made no particular case for the extension of slavery; his cause was the encouragement of unimpeded American expansion across the continent. He believed in the manifest destiny of the nation, a tendency he thought consistent with democracy; and his understanding of democracy embraced the unlimited power of a ruling majority to choose and change its mind and choose again. It was this enthusiastic faith that underlay the argument for popular sovereignty that Lincoln worked hard to refute in the 1850s. Douglas said he didn't care if people voted slavery up or down, and Lincoln often replied with a question: *can* you "not care" about a question as essential as slavery is to the understanding of moral right and wrong? Can you do so if you are possessed of emotions concerning any moral matter at all? If you are a person who has ever felt a conviction about anything, slavery, more than any other pattern of human conduct, would seem to prompt the emotion of conviction for or against.

Hence the importance of *saying* we are against slavery and the importance of hearing ourselves say it. This last emphasis is continuous and insistent in Lincoln, and it is peculiar to him. We learn (he seems to think) more profoundly what we believe when we hear ourselves say it. Such practice with the words of conviction hardens us for the conversion of words into deeds. When we persuade ourselves consciously and in line with our feelings—not involuntarily, as Satan does in *Paradise Lost* and Angelo in *Measure for Measure*, and not rationally and with enforced apathy, as Brutus does in his speech to the crowd in *Julius Caesar*; but by the deliberate work of the will—we will find that coming to know our conviction is nothing like saying "Thank you" and being certain the right message was conveyed. Lincoln's idea of persuasion, on the contrary, involves a consciousness of purpose, and a commitment to resist opposing purposes.

There are expressions of agreement and resolution so emphatic that the words involved enter the constitution of the act. Lincoln extends this idea, that our words have a grip on our deeds, in order to argue for the conscious strengthening of a momentous commitment. A promise broken is something like an aborted action; and regarding a person who cuts short his commitments in this way, our first and most significant response will simply be to wonder who he is. We do not go back to such people for a second try.

This rigorous understanding of the bond between our moral identity and what we hear ourselves say—though it sets an unforgiving standard of integrity—need not imply a contractual agreement between our reasons and the reasons of others who share our belief. We can be saying the same thing for different reasons, so long as in saying it we mean the same thing. In an improvised passage at the end of the published version of his Speech on the Kansas-Nebraska Act, Lincoln would deride the expectation that opponents of the extension of slavery should somehow catechize themselves and deliver a systematically unified argument:

> [Judge Douglas] says it is not quite fair to oppose him in this variety of ways. He should remember that he took us by surprise—astounded us—by this measure. We were thunderstruck and stunned; and we reeled and fell in utter confusion. But we rose each fighting, grasping whatever he could first reach—a scythe—a pitchfork—a chopping axe, or a butcher's cleaver. We struck in the direction of the sound; and we are rapidly closing in upon him. He must not think to divert us from our purpose, by showing us that our drill, our dress, and our weapons, are not entirely perfect and uniform.[11]

For Lincoln—and he has less interest here than Bagehot in any scientific claim—the cognitive and affective elements of conviction are indistinguishable. We hear an insult to our idea of human nature, or to the nature of the Union, and we rise up instinctively, as we would against an intruder in a nest or burrow.

To appreciate the force of Lincoln's utterance when he can seem most abstract and logical, we have to bear in mind his sense of the simplicity of the relevant emotion. The argument of the House Divided speech of June 1858 is compacted—as close to hardened and hurled conviction as any speech in the canon of political oratory—and its power to engender the emotions necessary for conflict is beyond doubt: it was this speech more than any other body of words that seemed to Americans of the time to lay down the probable cause of the war, if a civil war were to come. And here once again, one is faced by a difficult question about the degree of control any persuasive speaker can exert on the effect of his words.

No public declaration was ever more carefully meditated than the House Divided speech, and it confirms the accuracy of the characterization of Lincoln by his law partner and biographer William

Herndon: "Mr. Lincoln's perceptions were always cold, slow, logical, and exact." Still, one must ask: was the *form* of Lincoln's diagnosis as he perceived the state of the nation in 1858—so analytic in temper, so cold, slow, logical, and exact—was this not in itself a provocation?

> If we could first know *where* we are, and *whither* we are tending, we could then better judge *what* to do, and *how* to do it.
>
> We are now far into the *fifth* year, since a policy was initiated, with the *avowed* object, and *confident* promise, of putting an end to slavery agitation.
>
> Under the operation of that policy, that agitation has not only, *not ceased*, but has *constantly augmented*.
>
> In *my* opinion, it *will* not cease, until a *crisis* shall have been reached, and passed.
>
> "A house divided against itself cannot stand."
>
> I believe this government cannot endure, permanently half *slave* and half *free*.
>
> I do not expect the Union to be *dissolved*—I do not expect the house to *fall*—but I *do* expect it will cease to be divided.
>
> It will become *all* one thing, or *all* the other.
>
> Either the *opponents* of slavery, will arrest the further spread of it, and place it where the public mind shall rest in the belief that it is in course of ultimate extinction; or its *advocates* will push it forward, till it shall become alike lawful in *all* the states, *old* as well as *new*—*North* as well as *South*.
>
> Have we no *tendency* to the latter condition?[12]

Two separate strains of the argument, one cognitive, the other affective, are so subtly joined in this exordium that it may hard to see what is happening. "Only insofar as men are potentially free," Kenneth Burke wrote of the uses of political rhetoric, "must the spellbinder seek to persuade them. Insofar as they *must* do something, rhetoric is unnecessary, its work being done by the nature of things."[13] Lincoln puts his audience in the position of free citizens whose proper course of action is nevertheless determined by the nature of things.

We desire to know something, he says at the start. Where have the politics of our country placed us? And this is important, not as a topic of disinterested inquiry, but for the sake of rational mastery of ourselves and of our prospects. What we learn about "where we are" and about "whither we are tending" will immediately affect our understanding of what we now ought to do. The present and future, however, are guided most visibly by the recent past: the five years between 1853, which saw the start of the campaign to open the territories to slavery, and the moment in the summer of 1858 when Lincoln delivers this speech. The action of those years, as he initially reviews it, appears to have no agent: "a policy was inaugurated." Yet the policy has been fortified by beliefs, and we can see that it is a campaign to put an end not to slavery but to *agitation* over slavery. Four years earlier, in the Speech on the Kansas-Nebraska Act from which I quoted above, Lincoln had mocked the "lullaby arguments" that tended toward the accommodation of slavery without saying so. Political agitation may be salutary in the face of an unrelenting evil; but the intent of the present campaign is sedative: it means to blunt our ability to be made angry by a conspicuous moral wrong. The policy becomes all the more deceptive when it avows a general aim that many would reject if they could see it reduced to its logical constituents. Lincoln will attempt such a reduction in a later section of the speech where, with good circumstantial evidence, he accuses Douglas, along with Chief Justice Taney, the outgoing President Pierce, and the incoming President Buchanan, of having formed a conspiracy to nationalize slavery.[14] To put an end to anti-slavery agitation, as these men sought to do, meant, but did not acknowledge that it meant, to make the acceptance of slavery easier. Pro-slavery agitation would cease because the masters of the slave power would at last have been satisfied.

The next section of Lincoln's argument, in these short opening paragraphs, adopts the language of the composition and resolution of physical forces, which operate quite independent of such proddings of the will as are supplied by promises and vows. A free government will not *endure* to be half free and half slave, any more than an army could endure the command of two generals, each claiming total authority for every order that he issues. Lincoln in this way moves from the clear knowledge of physical states to the forming of probable social estimates, which, though they do refer to external realities, are rendered effectual only through a human agent. Lincoln himself *is* the relevant agent, but he has this peculiarity, that he does not say how he means to act. He passes from opinion to belief, from belief to expectation, and from expectation to confident prediction. "In *my* opinion," the agitation *"will* not cease, until a *crisis* shall have been reached, and passed." He believes that the country cannot endure half slave and half free; but he does not "expect" the house to fall. It will become all one or all the other—the house will move toward the coherence of a steady state, and it will become undivided for good or ill.

* * *

The House Divided speech has been as thoroughly analyzed as any speech in American history, with the exception of two others by Lincoln, both of them much shorter and less involved with consecutive argument. But though the tactics of the House Divided speech and its political bearings can be elucidated, up to a point, what resists analysis is its way of blending two idioms of description: the language of objective forces and that of human actors who are bearers of sentiments, beliefs, and expectations. Lincoln hoped to influence the *feelings* of his audience by this unusual combination of evoked authorities. He gambled that the result would be to plant a conviction about how to act in a consequential matter of right and wrong.

Evidently he believed that the two sorts of appeal could work together, instead of canceling each other's impact by the apparent incompatibility of the methods employed. Why might this be so? For Lincoln, the answer lay in the almost physical influence of conscious avowal on people's determination to act; and he would say so explicitly in the Cooper Institute Address of February 1860. The Southern states are unsatisfied when they hear disapproving words spoken of slavery, and they grow every day more resentful. "What will convince them?" asks Lincoln. "This, and this only: cease to call slavery *wrong*, and join them in calling it *right*. And this must be done thoroughly—done in *acts* as well as in *words*."[15] What we choose to call a thing matters effectively as a motive to action, and almost materially as a component of our actions. There are, in short, things done in words which, owing to their effects, must be counted as actions after all. Lincoln's belief that this is so may account for the insistence with which he marks his emphasis by italics: a practice unusual for him, but carried over from the House Divided speech to the sentences quoted above from the Cooper Institute Address.

Why, in a speech like Lincoln's at the Cooper Institute—delivered in a bid to be nominated for the presidency—should he have placed so much stock in the mere saying of the words "slavery is wrong"? The reason has to do with an imagining of the physical element in conviction, a belief carried from ourselves to ourselves. We are felt to act as witnesses of our own intention at the moment when it crystalizes. This suggests—contrary to the theory of prudential third-person sympathy in the moral philosophy of Smith—that words bear our signature in the same way that acts may do. Yet this can happen only when words prove by sequence, repetition, and mutual confirmation that they are intended as actions and not as accidental verbal events. Clearness, intensity, constancy, and interestingness all play a part among the necessary qualities of the emotion that drive our saying a difficult thing again and again. Once we recognize that we can hardly remain ourselves without saying the thing in question—that "slavery is wrong," for example—the pressure to say it acts on us with a force as compelling as a physical threat. A state of intense emotion, which cannot be entirely voluntary, is required even for the speaking of such a conviction. And it really commits us more than any promise could do. Our words of belief from emotion constitute a pledge that unavoidably takes us beyond words.

4

Persuasion and Responsibility

Yeats, Auden, Orwell

W. B. Yeats chose as an epigraph to *Responsibilities* an aphorism—"In dreams begins responsibility"—which he pretended to have borrowed from an "old play." Suppose we think of persuasion as a kind of dreaming aloud, which the dreamer asks other people to listen to and be somehow affected by. This lecture will discuss the relationship between two poets who did some of their dreaming aloud; and it will consider their respective views of the poet's responsibility for the effects such dreams may engender. I begin by marking at once a significant contrast and a continuity between the careers of Yeats and W. H. Auden.

The early Yeats exemplified an aestheticism that shunned in principle the rhetorical aim of changing the minds of readers or affecting their practical lives in any way. By the last two decades of his life, however, he was writing poems that came close to propaganda for aristocratic society, and he showed a relentless hostility toward enemies whom he was not shy of naming. Auden, in his last decades, claimed an exemplary civic function for art, a function that deliberately excluded any notion of pragmatic effect—a stance far closer to pure aestheticism than he was willing to acknowledge. And yet Auden had come to be known, through his early volumes of the 1930s, as the self-conscious leader of a poetic movement dedicated to political reform and possibly to revolution. Though they seem to have moved in opposite directions, therefore, I will look at these two poets together at a moment in the late 1930s and early 1940s when George Orwell wrote discerning commentaries on both. Orwell at this time had come to believe (as he says the experience of the Spanish Civil War convinced him) that serious literature could not escape having a political motive. Nor could it inoculate itself against having a persuasive effect.

* * *

In "Coole Park and Ballylee, 1931," Yeats has been contemplating emblems of nature and desire such as the swan: "That stormy white / But seems a concentration of the sky"—the image overwhelms him for a moment—"But in the morning's gone, no man knows why." Yeats is arrested by such images and bewildered when he searches for their significance. What is the peculiar quality of the soul? Can it be captured in an image? The poem does not answer those questions, but we hardly notice the fact. What holds our attention, in this poem and in others of his final decade, is the splendor of Yeats's description of the aristocratic culture he loves and the place of beauty it has made for itself:

> A spot whereon the founders lived and died
> Seemed once more dear than life; ancestral trees
> Or gardens rich in memory glorified
> Marriages, alliances and families,
> And every bride's ambition satisfied.
> Where fashion or mere fantasy decrees
> We shift about—all that great glory spent—
> Like some poor Arab tribesman and his tent.[1]

An impression of the ancient grandeur has stayed with him, a residue of memory:

> But all is changed, that high horse riderless,
> Though mounted in that saddle Homer rode
> Where the swan drifts upon a darkening flood.

A similar vision of catastrophe had formed the explicit background of "A Prayer for My Daughter," written more than a decade earlier:

> I have walked and prayed for this young child an hour
> And heard the sea-wind scream upon the tower,
> And under the arches of the bridge, and scream
> In the elms above the flooded stream;
> Imagining in excited reverie
> That the future years had come,
> Dancing to a frenzied drum,
> Out of the murderous innocence of the sea.

The future will bring democracy and all the detritus of the flood, but his daughter will be steadfast: "O may she live like some green laurel / Rooted in one dear perpetual place."

It is the appearance of innocence—a child asleep in a howling storm—that recalls to Yeats the lovely ways of an aristocracy. Those high-born manners comprehend the modesty and graciousness with which his daughter as a mature woman will eventually be endowed. Her virtue is to be discerned in her abstention from arrogant acts of the will and her innocence of the envy that may lead to such acts: "If there's no hatred in a mind / Assault and battery of the wind / Can never tear the linnet from the leaf." Being her father's daughter, she will naturally ally herself with the great things and the people her father stood with. This is a self-admiring posture, under the cover of humility and deference—a conventional stance with Yeats, and an effective one—yet its balance is upset by a detail near the end of the poem. Yeats there commends to his daughter the virtues of Nietzsche's Overman—the self-transcending genius of art and action who creates a culture out of himself and who need never ask forgiveness because he bears no grudge. Such a person deserves to be pardoned no matter what he may do: the aristocratic self prevails against memory and regret by discovering in itself a principle akin to that of the titled nobility:

> Considering that, all hatred driven hence,
> The soul recovers radical innocence
> And learns at last that it is self-delighting,
> Self-appeasing, self-affrighting,
> And that its own sweet will is Heaven's will.

Thus, what was lost in society by the processes of historical decay is recovered and redeemed by a soul that is fit to consecrate itself.

The same premonition of apocalypse, but now without any help from self-seclusion, was again Yeats's subject in "The Second Coming"—the prophetic poem that makes a public counterpart to the private wish of "A Prayer for My Daughter": "The blood-dimmed tide is loosed, and everywhere / The ceremony of innocence is drowned." The last line echoes "The murderous innocence of the sea," from "A Prayer for My Daughter"; but for all the resemblances between the private and the public poem about the coming terror, a strange discordance emerges—I don't think it is just a difference of shading—when one reads the two poems together. Innocence in a person is natural and may be sacred; anyway it is not artificial, if the idea means anything at all; whereas a "ceremony" is an artifice.

Can innocence be brought into being the way a title and a family name are passed on? If we think of Burke's lament for the age of chivalry—"that sensibility of principle, that chastity of honour, which felt a stain like a wound, which inspired courage whilst it mitigated ferocity"— perhaps it is credible to suppose that an aristocratic class in society could *create innocence*. After all, in order to appear to have earned the costume of virtue, noble men and women had actually to be high-minded, to a degree. You lose the enchantment of Yeats's conception here if you look hard at the doctrine; and yet the pathos of these two poems depends on an embrace of the doctrine: to grasp the form of the loss, we have ourselves to feel cheated of the ceremony of innocence, an artifice that became second nature to an enviable caste. The loss must inspire in us a horrified indignation at the ingenious lovely things that are gone. We are made to feel both an aesthetic and a moral injustice in the vanishing of the life of Coole Park and Ballylee—the love of beauty it fostered along with the characteristic acts of courage and magnanimity.

* * *

There is a cult of the "clean sweep" that must strike any close reader of Yeats's writings after 1918.[2] The mood strangely combines elegiac regret and an unembarrassed affinity with a power sufficiently muscular to remake the world—the monster that will destroy the destroyers of the old order that Yeats loved. A passage of *A Vision* that he liked well enough to quote in *On the Boiler* goes far to capture this feeling:

> Dear Predatory birds, prepare for war, prepare your children and all that you can reach. . . . Test art, morality, custom, thought, by Thermopylae, make rich and poor act so to one another that they can stand together there. Love war because of its horror, that belief may be changed, civilisation renewed. We desire belief and lack it. Belief comes from shock and is not desired.[3]

He means the shock of the forced acceptance of something terrible—the subject matter also of "Leda and the Swan."

Yeats was right about the modern aversion from the particular beliefs he favored: they were not desired and were feared for understandable reasons owing to the shock they caused. But it seems false to say that we "desire belief," if that implies, as Yeats wants it to imply, a system of belief, a religion or ideology. Rather—here I return to a formulation from the first lecture—we are hungry for beliefs and gravitate toward some of them; eventually, we find the ones we can adopt, or they find us. But there is no such thing as a desire to be possessed by belief-as-such. To think that there could be such a desire, however, is a natural inference from Nietzsche's analysis of modern nihilism, which Yeats by 1930 had entirely absorbed.

Again, in *On the Boiler*, he reflected on the new discipline he supposed would have to be forced on people once civilization suffered its latest catastrophic change: "Whenever we or our forefathers have been most Christian...we have been haunted by those faces dark with mystery, cast up by that other power that has ever more and more wrestled with ours, each living the other's death, dying the other's life."[4] The last great epochal change thus occurred with the demise of Christianity and the shedding of the doctrine of love which Christianity mistook for its own originating energy. A wish for destruction, primitive enough to connect us with the barbarians who overran the civilization that preceded Christian Europe, was in fact a central and acknowledged motive of Yeats's modernist ideology. We must expect to discover "those faces dark with mystery" in back of any supposed movement of enlightenment.

*   *   *

What were Auden's feelings when, in the late 1930s, he reckoned the degree to which he had once been an imitator of Yeats's style and a devotee of his moods and stances? The best help we can get in answering that question comes from Orwell's argument on the pervasiveness of "the political motive" in modernist writing of the 1930s. Over two months of the phony war of 1940, Orwell wrote one of his most adventurous essays, "Inside the Whale," which stands by itself in the criticism of the time. It offers a survey of the transition that brought English writing from its Georgian phase (which Orwell identifies with Housman as much as Wells and Shaw), through the major work of Joyce and Eliot, to the mood of commitment of the 1930s (which he finds in some ways uncongenial to literature). "Inside the Whale" is remembered partly now for its strictures on Auden's "Spain." I will focus on that part; but one needs to notice that the history recounted by Orwell adds up to a defense of the modernism of the 1920s, as represented by *Ulysses* but also by *Tropic of Cancer*. The anarchism of Henry Miller, anti-political as it is, Orwell here associates with an intimation of freedom. Two and a half years later, he would publish an essay on the poetry and personality of Yeats, an essay less well known but closely related to "Inside the Whale." It appeared in 1943, and Orwell chose to reprint it in his collection *Dickens, Dali, and Others*.

He had the nerve and sensibility to ask what might have caused the persistence of Yeats's influence through all the separate phases of twentieth-century writing discriminated in "Inside the Whale." Yeats's fame really did span the Georgian *and* the high modernist *and* the "committed" phase of literature, across the decades 1910–1940, with an authority that held strong for incompatible generations and tastes. Orwell shows much respect for Yeats's accomplishment, with a hint of the same underlying disgust that comes through in his estimate of Salvador Dali. He is particularly interested in the connection between style and political tendency: "One knows, for instance, that a Socialist would not write like Chesterton or a Tory imperialist like Bernard Shaw, though *how* one knows it is not easy to say. In the case of Yeats, there must be some kind of connection between his wayward, even tortured style of writing and his rather sinister vision of life."[5]

The connection is brought to a practical test by quotations: Yeats's artificiality, as a rule, says Orwell, "is accepted as Irishism"; he is even "credited with simplicity because he uses short words, but in fact one seldom comes on six consecutive lines of his verse in which there is not an archaism or an affected turn of speech." The details that follow make an interesting precedent for Yvor Winters's criticism of Yeats's style in *Forms of Discovery*, where a central charge against him, once more, would be affectation and unnaturalness. Orwell quotes from memory certain ecstatic or inspired passages that survive the posture of the style; but he has no doubt that, "translated into political terms, Yeats's tendency is Fascist. . . . Long before Fascism was ever heard of, he had had the outlook of those who reach Fascism by the aristocratic route."[6] And there follows a brief catalogue of his hatreds: democracy, science, and so on.

In the motives that drive Yeats, there seems to be a strain of perversity and cruelty: "The merely political Fascist claims always to be fighting for justice: Yeats, the poet, sees at a glance that Fascism means injustice, and acclaims it for that very reason."[7] Orwell goes on to speculate that Yeats's theory of recurring cycles must have fortified his disdain for any form of progress that might lift the lower orders; the details of the theory also cooperate with "the idea that knowledge must be a secret thing, limited to a small circle of initiates." He concludes by wishing that the book he is reviewing—*The Development of William Butler Yeats* by V. K. Narayana Menon—had gone further (even if speculatively) to associate modernist literature with a certain politics. "By and large the best writers of our time have been reactionary in tendency," says Orwell; "a writer's political and religious beliefs are not excrescences to be laughed away, but something that will leave their mark even on the smallest detail of his work."[8]

Auden's "Spain" had been the example brought up for similar analysis in "Inside the Whale"; and the coercive rhetoric of that poem seemed to Orwell as detached from right and wrong as the "tortured" grand style of Yeats. "Spain" was originally published as a pamphlet; it was clear, from the author's circumstances and known political views, that the poem was intended as republican propaganda; but it had a more specific purpose, namely to draw persons of courage and good will to *fight* on the republican side.

Certain ideas about world history and politics that such a reader could be expected to hold are briefly sketched or alluded to in the opening stanzas. All of these ideas turn on the contrast between Yesterday, when enterprises of great moment were possible to individuals in art, science, and religious practice, and Today, when the collective struggle for freedom and equality demands that each person subordinate his private will to the struggle. Yesterday all things tended toward enlightenment; the aim today must be to gain freedom for those who are not free; the mover of the change, as the closing lines will say, is History. And History is conceived of impersonally:

> Yesterday all the past. The language of size
> Spreading to China along the trade-routes; the diffusion
>   Of the counting-frame and the cromlech;
> Yesterday the shadow-reckoning in the sunny climates.[9]

And again:

> Yesterday the installation of dynamos and turbines,
> The construction of railways in the colonial desert;
>> Yesterday the classic lecture
> On the origin of Mankind. But to-day the struggle.

Having sketched this tapestry-like background, Auden imagines a voice calling out to the listener—the voice of whim or chance (it seems)—which blithely tells us that anything we may have wished to do we now may do. Evidently it is the voice of an imp or seducer, but in some way it also resembles the voice of the poet Auden. It does not appeal to a better part of ourselves; it only tells us what we already know. We must not doubt the power of this voice, but we must not blame it either. And at the moment of reading the poem, the word that comes from that voice is Spain:

> "What's your proposal? To build the just city? I will.
> I agree. Or is it the suicide pact, the romantic
>> Death? Very well, I accept, for
> I am your choice, your decision. Yes, I am Spain."

Up to this point, the tempter's voice has had a satirical or facetious cast. It will do anything we want—it may simply be another name for what we happen to want. But the tone here modulates to a more solemn register. There is a shift to a mannerly, confident, and quite determined rhetorical control, with an undertone of command—a posture that was characteristic of Auden at every stage of his career:

> Many have heard it on remote peninsulas,
> On sleepy plains, in the aberrant fisherman's islands
>> Or the corrupt heart of the city,
> Have heard and migrated like gulls or the seeds of a flower.
>
> They clung like birds to the long expresses that lurch
> Through the unjust lands, through the night, through the alpine tunnel;
>> They floated over the oceans;
> They walked the passes. All presented their lives.
>
> On that arid square, that fragment nipped off from hot
> Africa, soldered so crudely to inventive Europe;
>> On that tableland scored by rivers,
> Our thoughts have bodies; the menacing shapes of our fever

Are precise and alive. For the fears which made us respond
To the medicine ad. and the brochure of winter cruises
        Have become invading battalions;
And our faces, the institute-face, the chain-store, the ruin

Are projecting their greed as the firing squad and the bomb.
Madrid is the heart. Our moments of tenderness blossom
        As the ambulance and the sandbag;
Our hours of friendship into a people's army.

In the course of these stanzas a political conversion is taking place.
The republican volunteers from abroad are at first portrayed as
having the properties of animals or plants, things without conscious
will or intellect: they are like gulls, like seeds, like birds, like seaweed.
But arriving in Spain, they are transformed. Their slothful wishes
and dreadful fantasies materialize in the form of the Fascist enemy;
their strength of purpose and magnanimity are embodied in the
work of resistance to Fascism and generous aid to the Republic.
"Our moments of tenderness blossom / As the ambulance and the
sandbag." Ordinary actions, by virtue of their engagement in this
battle, come to represent a sort of commissioned labor that builds up a
kingdom of ends.

The final stanzas of the poem depict a landscape charged with a
fresh purpose. It is now as if we who read the poem have joined the
army. The contrast is no longer between yesterday, with its leisure and
fulfillment, and today with its uncertainties. Now the point of view is
entirely from today; it looks practically and not fancifully at tomorrow,
when there will be time to love, think, and live for ourselves.

* * *

I regret the propagandistic fluency of that last sentence, but the poem
itself is propaganda for a vision of revolutionary progress, and it
shouldn't be purged of its character in polite paraphrase that avoids
the clichés in evidence. The poem speaks for a hope that remains
necessarily vague. The romantic wish cannot be satisfied, where we
stand today, since the imperative is unity in the cause. The force of this
imperative overrides every individual nuance and scruple. Today we
must do things we would rather not do, and we are willing that our
acts should appear anonymous:

To-morrow for the young the poets exploding like bombs,
The walks by the lake, the winter of perfect communion;
    To-morrow the bicycle races
Through the suburbs on summer evenings. But to-day the struggle.

To-day the deliberate increase in the chances of death,
The conscious acceptance of guilt in the necessary murder;
    To-day the expending of powers
On the flat ephemeral pamphlet and the boring meeting.

To-day the makeshift consolations: the shared cigarette,
The cards in the candlelit barn, and the scraping concert,
    The masculine jokes; to-day the
Fumbled and unsatisfactory embrace before hurting.

The stars are dead. The animals will not look.
We are left alone with our day, and the time is short, and
    History to the defeated
May say Alas but cannot help nor pardon.

The power of those closing lines can still be felt these many decades later. But there is a contradiction within the emotion that has been so carefully worked up.

The volunteer in the Spanish Republican cause was at first pictured as a luxury-loving dupe, an ordinary sensual man interested in the latest inventions and what to do on his next holiday. Only the imperative of Spain can transform him; but under its impress, his life will find meaning in company with others in the cause. Yet at the end—it is a curious element in the morale of the poem—he has gone back to being the passive executor of an alien will; only, now he is under the command of forces he recognizes and approves of. Even so, the "you" of the poem, the reader, the volunteer for Spain, by the end is as much estranged from the conduct of freedom as he was at the beginning. For how can freedom show itself if not by self-chosen work toward a chosen end? The reader-volunteer, on the contrary, submits to the will of external forces and does so with a fatalistic obedience. The cause is larger than he is; it rightly defines him; the determinations of the cause are felt to be at once authoritative and extra-moral: his own actions are those of an animate instrument and not a moral agent. He consents to the justice by which a force greater than himself can compel him to act.

Orwell, who unlike Auden fought in Spain, felt the tremendous appeal of the poem, but he heard it from a sufficient distance to notice what sort of persuasion it was driving at. "Look, for instance," wrote Orwell, "at this extract from Mr Auden's poem 'Spain' (incidentally this poem is one of the few decent things that have been written about the Spanish war)"; and quoting the three stanzas that begin "To-morrow for the young the poets exploding like bombs," he makes a comment that has become almost as famous as the poem:

> The second stanza is intended as a sort of thumbnail sketch of a day in the life of a "good party man". In the morning a couple of political murders, a ten-minutes' interlude to stifle "bourgeois" remorse, and then a hurried luncheon and a busy afternoon and evening chalking walls and distributing leaflets. All very edifying. But notice the phrase "necessary murder". It could only be written by a person to whom murder is at most a *word*. Personally I would not speak so lightly of murder. It so happens that I have seen the bodies of numbers of murdered men—I don't mean killed in battle, I mean murdered. Therefore I have some conception of what murder means—the terror, the hatred, the howling relatives, the post-mortems, the blood, the smells. To me, murder is something to be avoided. So it is to any ordinary person. The Hitlers and Stalins find murder necessary, but they don't advertise their callousness, and they don't speak of it as murder; it is "liquidation", "elimination" or some other soothing phrase. Mr Auden's brand of amoralism is only possible if you are the kind of person who is always somewhere else when the trigger is pulled.[10]

A strong accusation, and one that the poem is not equipped to deal with. Notice, too, the marked similarity to Orwell's charge against Yeats: where the "merely political" oppressor hides the wrong by resorting to euphemism, the poet backs his claim to realism by endorsing the wrong outright. One can only say in extenuation, if it does extenuate, that Auden's call to self-sacrifice without illusion involves an act of *abstraction*, which this poem will be found to share with many other calls to a purposeful sacrifice. The speaker in such a setting is compelled to exalt the act of self-suppression by comparing his obedience to a natural force, or by merging it with a collective will that looks like a natural force.

*   *   *

Auden's elegy on the death of Yeats in 1939 seems to have been written as if he knew that strictures like those I just quoted from Orwell were in fact going to be leveled against him as well as Yeats. I will be treating "In Memory of W.B. Yeats" as the summing up of a three-sided argument that in some ways answers Orwell, but I should make it clear that the chronological order runs differently: "Spain" (1937), "In Memory of W. B. Yeats" (1939), "Inside the Whale" (1940). Two quite distinct motives—delivered so casually we can fail to see how much they matter to Auden—are brought together in his elegy for Yeats. There is a hope that words, engendered by poetic imagination, may somehow be exempt from the burden of moral responsibility, because they do not mean to persuade. And there is a self-protective defense against the fear that sometimes words may actually make things happen.

Auden writes as an artist instructing us in an intricate truth that lies outside the usual walks of belief and persuasion. We are asked to consider what it might be to respect a work of art as something good in itself. More particularly, Auden is conscious of offering his apology for Yeats from the standpoint of one whose prophecies of "death of the old gang" had made him known as anything but a defender of art for art's sake. He begins with the sparest of neutral observations; the poet has died, and the non-human world cannot grieve:

> He disappeared in the dead of winter:
> The brooks were frozen, the airports almost deserted,
> And snow disfigured the public statues;
> The mercury sank in the mouth of the dying day.
> O all the instruments agree
> The day of his death was a dark cold day.

The strange lines that follow soon after—"By mourning tongues / The death of the poet was kept from his poems"—suggest that the rituals of memorializing may insulate us from actual grief; and something like this is true of the sanctity we throw around the words of poems: they keep us from quite taking in the humanity of the poet. "But for him it was his last afternoon as himself," Auden's elegy continues, "An afternoon of nurses and rumours."

At the moment of his death, the poet turned into something greater, but he lost any protection his irony may once have afforded against the imposition of meaning by external forces: "The current of his feeling failed: he became his admirers." Auden continues this train of thought with a matter-of-fact notation of the dead poet's helplessness:

> Now he is scattered among a hundred cities
> And wholly given over to unfamiliar affections;
> To find his happiness in another kind of wood
> And be punished under a foreign code of conscience.
> The words of a dead man
> Are modified in the guts of the living.

Even so, writes Auden (who two years before had dismissed the claims of both tomorrow and yesterday): "in the importance and noise of to-morrow . . . A few thousand will think of this day / As one thinks of a day when one did something slightly unusual." It is a vein of calculated understatement well suited to a moment of public and ceremonial humility. The connection between word and deed—between the composer of words and the performer of actions—is touched upon delicately here. Yeats's readers will think of this day as one thinks of a day when one *did* something unusual. As the poet's words left an enduring impression on the reader, so the reader is prompted to leave an impression on life; and by that vicarious transfer of responsibility, the aesthetic effect of poetry comes to seem the reader's own. It belongs to one's experience as surely as if it were something one had done.

The elegy continues to render the occasion smaller than the death of the greatest living British poet would seem to warrant. The all-too-human word "silly," for example, is brought in to diminish Yeats to an affectionate size, but the trick is lightly done and escapes any charge of frivolity:

> You were silly like us: your gift survived it all;
> The parish of rich women, physical decay,
> Yourself; mad Ireland hurt you into poetry.
> Now Ireland has her madness and her weather still,
> For poetry makes nothing happen: it survives
> In the valley of its saying where executives
> Would never want to tamper; it flows south
> From ranches of isolation and the busy griefs,
> Raw towns that we believe and die in; it survives,
> A way of happening, a mouth.

Here I have to point out—a thing one often finds in confronting a rhetorician of supreme cunning—that the most ordinary word of the passage is the word that dares most and ought most to be questioned.

The word is *for*. "For poetry makes nothing happen." If we agree that poetry makes nothing happen, the proof must be that all the things Yeats's poetry might have changed, modified, softened, prevented, or obliterated are already showing how they were untouched by his poetry. Thus Yeats contributed to the nationalism and folkworship which are part of what Auden has in mind when he speaks of "mad Ireland" (though one may judge that mad Ireland helped rather than "hurt" Yeats into poetry). Poetry cannot change the weather or put off bodily decrepitude; but the parish of rich women were not a bane or a curse on a level with such irremediable circumstances. The truth is that Yeats embraced rather than merely endured the conditions that Auden mentions. The word "silly," it turns out, is doing a great deal of work to justify that "For." Yeats was silly to want to improve things, but the poem throws up its hands: what can one say? He was insufficiently prepared and he had his infatuations. Auden passes over the faults in a tone that approaches pity but stops short; after all, he was silly *like us*. The effect of that insinuating phrase is to build up a confiding fellowship in the smaller sins.[11]

* * *

To show how craftily the elegy works to vindicate Yeats with materials that might be used to condemn him, one need only compare Auden's fascinating prose dialogue on the same subject, "The Public v. the Late Mr. W. B. Yeats," which he sent to *Partisan Review* shortly after the poem was completed in the spring of 1939. "Silly" would have seemed a blamable understatement in this setting, given the simple accuracy of the prosecutor's charge:

> For the great struggle of our time to create a juster social order, he felt nothing but the hatred which is born of fear. It is true that he played a certain part in the movement for Irish Independence, but ... of all the modes of self-evasion open to the well-to-do, Nationalism is the easiest and most dishonest.[12]

On the other hand, as Edward Mendelson has pointed out, "the name of the case—The Public v. the Late Mr. W. B. Yeats—is subtly different from the names of cases tried in English-speaking courts. Yeats is being accused not by the Crown or the People but by a category for which Auden never in his life had a good word, the *Public*."[13] If there are two honorable sides to the conflict between aesthetic and moral value which the poem confronts, Auden would take care to guard himself redundantly on both sides.

The third section of the elegy means to recognize the force of the prosecutor's criticism. It circumvents the difficulty by applauding the survival of poetry as a miracle in itself. All human beings, because we all use language, are finally the beneficiaries of that survival:

> Earth, receive an honoured guest;
> William Yeats is laid to rest:
> Let the Irish vessel lie
> Emptied of its poetry.

Here, as at the start, the poet is "kept from" his poetry, but the action has changed from mourning the death of a man to celebrating the value of his poems:

> Time that is intolerant
> Of the brave and innocent,
> And indifferent in a week
> To a beautiful physique,
>
> Worships language and forgives
> Everyone by whom it lives;
> Pardons cowardice, conceit,
> Lays its honours at their feet.
>
> Time that with this strange excuse
> Pardoned Kipling and his views,
> And will pardon Paul Claudel,
> Pardons him for writing well.

It is a sort of allegory: time worships, time forgives, while shallow or petulant human creatures look on bewildered and somehow obliged to assent. The pure and gifted use of words has a value akin to the presence of grace; if sins have been committed, the medium of absolution is that impersonal element, Time, which cannot be accused of the human imperfections of a poet's admirers. Though Auden would later say, in a mood of stern mockery, that Shelley's description of poets as "the unacknowledged legislators of the world" was really a description of the secret police, it is remarkable that he here awards Yeats his reprieve with a close echo of the argument of Shelley's *Defence of Poetry*: the errors of poets "have been weighed and found to have been dust in the balance; if their sins were as scarlet, they are now white as snow: they have been washed in the blood of the mediator and the redeemer, Time." But Auden outdoes Shelley in ascribing to this agent of redemption a power at once human and godlike. Time worships language because it knows the immortality of language: something no person or generation can know. As for the poet himself—that is, Yeats, the fallible mortal—Auden may now be felt to say that his words persuaded without coercion. He was constrained only by the necessities of poetic form and the imaginative exclusions that are the other side of imaginative freedom:

> Follow, poet, follow right
> To the bottom of the night,
> With your unconstraining voice
> Still persuade us to rejoice.

Through the execution of a purpose in words, the poet was able to create joy—a feeling nothing else but music can create in a comparable way; but a suggestion of conscious will is carried by the word "persuade," which would not be allowed to pass in a description of music.

The final reward of poetry, this poem argues, is relief from a parching emptiness that is the opposite of joy, and the recognition of a kind of freedom in the midst of servitude. By the words of the poet, which now have been reunited with the poet himself, we are taught not doctrine and not a therapy of specific feeling, but how to praise. Since this implies some previous knowledge of the things that deserve praise, the poet, even a poet of partly narrow or deleterious views like Yeats or Kipling or Claudel, teaches over his own head. The words know a kind of perfection—which can only be good, only a cause of gratitude—beyond what the maker of the words could consciously and personally embody:

> In the deserts of the heart
> Let the healing fountain start,
> In the prison of his days
> Teach the free man how to praise.

* * *

I want to pause now to take in a general puzzle about the argument of the poem—the thing that makes it so hard to say what it is trying to persuade us *of.* The elegy is full of a pleading that wants not to be seen as special pleading; but if we reduce it to a semblance of logical form, the three sections make very disparate impressions. The first part tells us that the poet can't be reduced to his words: he is strangely separate from them, and even more separate from the readers and admirers who after his death will become the inevitable bearers of the meaning of those words. Posthumously, he will be punished under a foreign code of conscience—scattered among the hundred cities where he is read (and read now as an alien, since he no longer controls the meaning of his words). But could Yeats, could any poet, ever control the meaning of his words while he was alive? The opening section of Auden's elegy must turn on this contrast, but the poem begs the question of whether the contrast is true. The lesson in this part anyway appears to be the helplessness of the words of the poet. They can do nothing for him now, and he can do nothing for them. The passage from a condition so alive to a condition so entirely unknown takes place, as one may feel it should, on "a dark cold day."

The second section is more directly persuasive in technique. It forgives Yeats and makes his faults or sins eminently pardonable. If his poetry did wrong, we cannot blame his poetry: "For poetry makes nothing happen." We value poetry, to say it again, as a gesture of pure communication which tells us something about the world without exactly imparting information or asking us to do anything. Executives may want to tamper, Ireland may go mad, but poetry has no such tendency or direction. It is "A way of happening, a mouth."

How extreme is this picture of the insulation of art from practical effects! And in fact the history of the poem's composition shows that Auden was aware of the strangeness of going to this length to prove the innocence of an art. The second section was written and inserted last; in its original appearance, in *The New Republic*, the elegy had passed from the first to the third section with no intervening matter. But a favorite stratagem of Auden's for defying his own doubts was always to make his counterstatement against them as radical as possible. Almost the last word of the counsel for the defense, in his prose dialogue on Yeats, refers to "the fallacious belief that art ever makes anything happen, whereas the honest truth...is that, if not a poem had been written, not a picture painted, not a bar of music composed, the history of man would be materially unchanged."[14] The hedge-word in that sentence is "materially": the adverb deprives the assertion of practical value, since Auden never believed that human nature, or indeed human progress, could be brought completely under material measure. Let us then deny him the use of "materially" and ask what it means to say, without sophistication, that in the absence of the arts that he names, the history of humankind would be unchanged.

How odd it seems to suppose that—alone among all human pursuits and productions—the work of artists can be relied on to have *no* effect. But since it is undeniable that works of art do affect people emotionally, the additional premise required to render the sentence true must be: that our emotions do not affect our actions; or, that emotions properly sublimated in the medium of art do not escape and touch us in practical ways. But what could be the property belonging to art that ensures this sort of illicit influence will not occur? There is no such property. The enchantment of art owes something to the understanding that it is a game, as the later Auden never failed to emphasize; yet something about the game continues in our minds after the players have done. This residue or carry-over cannot be separated from human action in the non-fictive world.

Yeats, it must be said, was in some moods less forgiving toward himself. "Did that play of mine send out / Certain men the English shot?" A fair question. Auden, by contrast, is solemn in issuing a reprieve to the poet on account of the survival of his poems. And notice how the word *survive* is repeated. The force of the repetition draws on etymology: the poet through his words has a life on top of life, and may properly enjoy an afterlife different from anything that happens to other men and women. Poetry is a form of action without content. Symbolic action, let us call it, without a pragmatic end. A way of happening.

With the third section of the poem, we pass to yet another species of vindication and memorial. Divided now from the corruptible body of the poet, the words of his poetry are emptied out of the vessel that contained them. In a world distorted by hatred and preparing for war, with inhabitants cut off from each other like prisoners, each in his separate cell, the words of the poet will retire after his death and turn away from war to farming, from epic to georgic, from the instigation of death to the production of life. The words, on behalf of the poet, will do this because of nothing especially virtuous in the poet himself, but just because that is what great poetry does: it purifies the language of the tribe (in the phrase of Stéphane Mallarmé which Auden may well have had in mind). But Auden also seems to say that Yeats, the fallible person, was generous in a manner that prefigured the fecundity of his words. He made an emotion akin to joy from the energy with which he cursed. He sang of failure, including his own; of "human unsuccess / In a rapture of distress." Yeats, however, is praised most of all because, by the faithful pursuit of his calling, he has given a voice to human freedom. So this elegy for a poet whose politics were by no means hostile to Fascism very nearly ends as an overt appeal against Fascism.

To abstract the argument very rapidly: part one—the poet's words are no longer his own, so he cannot be praised or blamed for the good or harm they did; part two—his words cannot have done either good or harm, since poetry makes nothing happen; part three—poetry as great as Yeats's does make something happen, after all; it makes us rejoice, leads us into rapture, assists in a kind of healing. Without the man ever having set anything like a good example, the poems that he wrote are exemplary. By itself, this conclusion offers the least sentimental of all justifications for art. The eloquence is Auden's own; the argument is one that not only Shelley but Emerson and Blake had expounded before him. But we are not quite allowed to interpret the conclusion as if it stood alone.

I have laid out the progression diagrammatically, which is not the way any reader coming upon Auden's elegy a first, second, or third time would experience it, but the outline may show how an obscure momentum works through shades of feeling that bear a semblance of argument. The absence of logical connection is made more tractable too by the distinct meters and rhetorical conventions that are enforced in the separate sections. Part one is loosely accentual pentameter, and reads as if spoken by a chorus in a verse drama. Part two is close to prose notation, done in loose syllabics (between 20 and 24 syllables every two lines). Part three, tight and austere, reads as a benediction.

* * *

It seems that we were convinced of something here. What could that be? The sentence "Poetry makes nothing happen" is true if and only if poetry makes nothing happen. Yet the poem we have just read has persuaded us to imagine a character and a predicament in a certain way. This poem indeed makes something happen. It vindicates the overriding good faith of *intentions* in the artist, or rather, in the artistic essence of the artist, which is separable from the admittedly confused human purposes and mixed motives of W. B. Yeats. The elegy may have the additional effect of vindicating "Spain" and certain other poems Auden had published in the 1930s. Yet it is honest enough to signal its own doubt even while triumphing over the reader's initial doubt. The verse of Auden's final section, composed as it is in four-beat couplets, imitates the pattern of some of Yeats's most scandalous and unpardonable lines from "Under Ben Bulben." Auden may write "In the deserts of the heart, / Let the healing fountain start"—that is the melody—but the measure comes from elsewhere:

> You that Mitchel's prayer have heard,
> "Send war in our time, O Lord!"
> Know that when all words are said
> And a man is fighting mad,
> Something drops from eyes long blind,
> He completes his partial mind.

So Auden's poem for Yeats calls up, in a meter used by the dead poet, the pitiless cry for war which the living poet will not allow to mean what it says.

Probably the right way to take "In Memory of W. B. Yeats" is to see it as a serious game about belief. It looks at how we think of belief from various angles, and asks whether an art of words, being incapable of persuasion, can free itself of the responsibilities that go with belief—the responsibilities, too, that go with willful attempts by a speaker to escape blame for an influence on other people that he actively sought. Auden hoped that there could be such an art of freedom. You teach the free man how to praise while remaining exempt from complicity in the effect of your own words. He would like to believe in such a freedom, but the structure itself of "In Memory of W. B. Yeats" shows the difficulty of sustaining the belief. The poem is written to espouse the consoling but false hope that verbal art can be an epitome of pure play, an enactment of wonder and pleasure by which we are uniquely humanized.

Words make things happen, though in the case of literature—and I would add, in the case of any discursive text—it is a long reach and an unprofitable speculation to wonder how they perform certain actions by virtue of their saying. They make things happen uncontrollably, unspecifiably. And in the presence of great writing, for that reason, it is appropriate for us to fear as well as admire even those words whose greatness we recognize. Because the drift of persuasion is never identical with the aim of imagination, and because imagination itself is partly involuntary, our knowledge of the mere fact that we admire certain words will always be surer than our knowledge of the plausible reasons to fear them.

5

What Are We Allowed to Say?

Rushdie, Mill, Savio

Free speech is an aberration—it is best to begin by admitting that. In most societies throughout history and in all societies some of the time, censorship has been the means by which a ruling group or a visible majority cleanses the channels of communication to ensure that certain conventional practices will go on operating undisturbed. It is not only traditional cultures that see the point of taboos on speech and expressive action. Even in societies where faith in progress is part of a common creed, censorship is often taken to be a necessary means to effect improvements that will convey a better life to all. Violent threats like the fatwa on Salman Rushdie and violent acts like the assassinations at *Charlie Hebdo* remind us that a militant religion is a dangerous carrier of the demand for the purification of words and images. Meanwhile, since the fall of Soviet communism, liberal bureaucrats in the North Atlantic democracies have kept busy constructing speech codes and guidelines on civility to soften the impact of unpleasant ideas. Is there a connection between these various developments?

Probably an inbred trait of human nature renders the attraction of censorship perennial. Most people (the highly literate are among the worst) believe that what is good for them will be good for others. Besides, a regime of censorship must claim to derive its authority from settled knowledge and not opinion. Once enforcement and exclusion have done their work, this assumption becomes almost irresistible; and it is relied on to produce a fortunate and economical result: self-censorship. We stay out of trouble by gagging ourselves. Among the few motives that may strengthen the power of resistance is the consciousness of having been deeply wrong oneself, either regarding some abstract question or in personal or public life. Another motive of resistance occasionally pitches in: a radical, quasi-physical horror of seeing people coerce other people without having to supply reasons. For better or worse, this second motive is likely to be mixed with misanthropy.

As far back as one can trace the vicissitudes of public speech and its suppression, the case for censorship seems to have begun in the need for strictures against blasphemy. The introductory chapter of *Blasphemy*, by the great American legal scholar Leonard Levy, covers "the Jewish trial of Jesus"; it is followed in close succession, in Levy's account, by the Christian invention of the concept of heresy and the persecution of the Socinian and Arminian heretics and later of the Ranters, Antinomians, and early Quakers. After an uncertain interval of state prosecutions and compromises in the nineteenth century, Levy's history closes at the threshold of a second Enlightenment in the mid-20th: the endorsement by the North Atlantic democracies of a regime of almost unrestricted freedom of speech and expression.

Writing in the early 1990s, Levy gave a final chapter to the Rushdie affair. He couldn't be sure if this was a dénouement or the start of a separate history. It was anyway a sort of return. The very idea of regulating speech had been engendered by conflict with the religious strictures on blasphemy: "That freedom of conscience came at all to Christendom was probably the result of perpetual religious fission: the promptings of conscience that seized people to their innermost depths varied so much that freedom was possible for none unless for all."[1] Enlightenment universalism, in short, did not yield the imperative of freedom without the clash of parochial forces interested in the limitation of freedom. Nor has "cultural pluralism" weakened the appetite for suppression among the mixed cultures of the West.

* * *

A few sticking points remain, even for the most liberal-minded technocrats: the legality of circulating child pornography, for example, or of denying the facts of the Holocaust. In the first case, the clear offence is that children cannot know the meaning of consenting to appear in a sex film, and it is a crime to make money from actions that are already criminal. The same goes for sharing copies of such a film, since distribution abets the crime. It is harder to say what sanction ought to apply against the person who downloads the illegal video but keeps it on a private computer. In America, the Fourth Amendment gives security to the citizen against unreasonable searches and seizures. Is a person to be judged culpable who has spent several hours on an illegal pornographic site? What about several minutes, or several seconds, initially by accident? An endless vista of prosecution is opened for a regime that turns its energy against activities that range from the abominable to the merely unsavory.

In the case of Holocaust denial—the crime for which David Irving was sentenced to three years in prison and banned from returning to Austria—the fear of contagion in some countries is based on rational horror instructed by recent experience. That is the argument for making an exception to the belief that the truth will always win out in a fair contest. But the exception is unsettling. The doctrine that truth in an open debate has nothing to fear from falsehood had been supposed to apply above all to truths about historical events and new theories in the natural sciences. The sanction against Holocaust denial treats grown-ups—the gullible audience of the false claim—as children not yet in possession of their mature faculties. Many Europeans, it is supposed, were so effectively brainwashed two generations ago that, even now, they and their offspring cannot risk any exposure to falsehoods of a certain kind. They lack the mental resources to resist the intoxication. This pattern of enforcement presumably will not last for ever. When the Holocaust becomes a more distant memory—perhaps a century from now—the idea of denying that it took place will seem merely bizarre.

These partial exceptions apply to the sort of representation that many regard as a violent stimulant to weak minds. It is a narrow category and shows no sign of expanding. By contrast, the pressure to ban or denounce *The Satanic Verses* came from sensitivity to the feelings of an audience that would never be tempted to read it. The charge was no less imposing for that; the book was said to cause an injury, a wound—the relevant claim is that wrong words or gestures can amount to aggressive misrepresentation or "misrecognition." *The Satanic Verses*, in one of its multiple stories, showed the invention of a religion by a prophet whose visions are distorted by a satirist and a trickster scribe. The result is a scripture that counterfeits Islam. In the relationship between the prophet and his satirist and scribe, the latter pair enjoy a secret ascendancy. The iconoclasm of the novel was thus secured by an unreliable narrator, an unreliable story planted by the narrator, and a religious pretender made ridiculous by a claim of authority conferred by the story alone. The word of God, as conveyed by his spokesman on earth, comes to be altered, twisted, transposed and revised at pleasure by a worldly author no different in kind from a novelist or a playwright. The Higher Criticism has never been absorbed over large tracts of fundamentalist Islam any more than in evangelical Christianity; and the charge of blasphemy became the obvious method for interpreting the shock administered by Rushdie's novel.

Margaret Thatcher declined to prosecute *The Satanic Verses* for blasphemy; and once the fatwa was issued Rushdie was accorded police protection from the extraordinary threat. Still, the cravenness of the early reactions has not yet been forgotten. The novel was initially banned in Canada, and US bookstores were slow to risk the title on their shelves. Cautionary words about the need for sensitivity were uttered by academic as well as priestly authorities. "We respect each other's religious beliefs," wrote Syed Shahabuddin, who led the campaign to ban *The Satanic Verses* in India. "We do not intentionally outrage the religious feelings of others or insult their religion or ridicule the personalities to whom we are emotionally attached or mock our religious susceptibility." The Chief Rabbi of the United Kingdom, Immanuel Jakobovits, emphatically concurred: it was wrong to "tolerate a form of denigration and ridicule which can only breed resentment." In an essay on "Religious Anger and Minority Rights," Tariq Modood, the director of Bristol University's Centre for the Study of Ethnicity and Citizenship, wrote that "the group which feels hurt is the ultimate arbiter of whether a hurt has taken place." [2] On this view, to experience the feeling is to suffer the injury.

* * *

Rushdie's defenders were on solid ground when they invoked his right to publish a book that could elicit a plausible charge of blasphemy. Christopher Hitchens spoke early and courageously on those lines. "Behind the use of bleating words like 'offensive,'" he wrote in his *Nation* column on March 13, 1989, "one can sense abject *trahison*: the ecumenicism of the philistines"; as for conciliation or compromise, "it would be suicidal to suppose that any concession made to the superstitious will ever be the last." But the odd appearance of the word "philistine" in such a strictly political context turned the argument from a libertarian defense of publication to an aesthetic defense of the contents of the book—a sign of things to come. On the cable network C-Span, on February 21, 1989, Hitchens broadened his criticism:

> Tomorrow, shopping malls of the United States, which contain now one third of the book outlets in this country, will, of their own volition, not sell that book, because they are scared of a foreign despot... To be scared of a crazy foreign tyrant in this way is a really serious challenge to what we think of as the safe assumption of free speech and free inquiry, free expression and the necessity to defend it.

For Hitchens, denunciation of the cowardice of the merchants was not enough. He was speaking during a phone-in program, and as the calls from people in sympathy with offended Muslims piled up, he must have seen that his defense of the novel would be stronger if Rushdie's intentions were found to be salubrious. A full-throated endorsement followed: "I have read the book," he now said, and "I am clear in my mind that no insult to the Prophet, or to those who believe in the God of whom he is the messenger, is intended. The words that are complained of are spoken by a sick man, suffering from paranoid schizophrenia, in a dream in which he believes himself to be the archangel Gabriel." And again, and further: "The remarks [in the novel] made about religion are all carefully judged remarks about dogma—about people who have automatic, unthinking faith—and no one who has any genuine, devotional attachment to any religion could be offended." His friendship with Rushdie doubtless played a part, but it would have been better for honesty and good sense to withhold a bill of health that cleared the book and its author at a stroke. We don't defend the right to publish offensive words because we think the author well-meaning. The point is that we distrust the ambition of those who would take away the right more than we distrust the character of those who write or speak recklessly.

An echo of the aesthetic defense of Rushdie could be heard in Ian McEwan's retrospective comment on the affair in the *Guardian* on September 14, 2012: "it seemed like the social glue of multicultural-ism was melting away. We were coming apart, and doing it over a postmodern multi-layered satirical novel." What work is being performed in that sentence by the adjectives "postmodern" and "multi-layered"? Something like what Hitchens had in mind when he fell back on the word "philistine." McEwan went on to recall (with uncertain irony) how Rushdie himself "in a hopeful attempt to accommodate his opponents... spoke of his faith, or lack of it, as a God-shaped hole." Consider the words closely: a God-shaped hole. Rushdie, it seems, came up with his own "postmodern multi-layered" trope of negative theology to meet the terms of his orthodox accusers, but the imams would not credit his explanation. Should we? The libertarian argument in support of publishing *The Satanic Verses* had been simple and radical: any book deserves protection from censorship. The sentimental secondary argument pressed by defenders of the book—that its satire originated in faith (of a sort) as deep as orthodoxy—was constructed by unbelievers to assist the image of unbelievers.

* * *

The Rushdie affair set the pattern for the Western reaction to the terrorist attack on *Charlie Hebdo*. Perhaps because of the precedent, the grounds of defense in 2015 shifted at a faster pace, from straightforward political affirmation of press liberty to a claim for the moral courage and stature of the artists. At the same time, the question that had lingered for 25 years—whether aesthetic "framing" could somehow purge the noxious elements of a work—grew harder to answer in the case of satirical drawings that never pretended to the complexity of a postmodern novel. Rushdie for his part now abjured the piety of the God-shaped hole and any regard for "genuine, devotional attachment." In an English PEN statement for *Charlie Hebdo* on January 7, 2015, he spoke out frankly for impiety: "Religion, a medieval form of unreason, when combined with modern weaponry becomes a real threat to our freedoms." The solidarity appropriate to believers in free speech was made to mesh with a defense of satire as an artistic mode: "I stand with *Charlie Hebdo*, as we all must, to defend the art of satire, which has always been a force for liberty and against tyranny, dishonesty and stupidity."[3] Rushdie here went much further than his defenders had done in 1989; and what he was saying was not true. The publication of a satire of real persons is obviously consistent with freedom, and one can go further: toleration of satire itself is evidence that a culture of free expression is thriving. But a great proportion of satire in all ages has been directed by the haughty against the low and mean; consider the conduct of Alexander Pope toward his inferior

Colley Cibber in *The Dunciad.* Satire may come from the palace as well as the gutter. Nor does it serve reliably as an antidote to dishonesty and stupidity. It may answer stupidity with mischief and pretense with ridicule, but its weapons are wielded in a cause whose motives have rarely been single-minded. What could it mean to appreciate *Scoop* or *Sweeney Agonistes* as a contribution to the fight for liberty against tyranny? Yet these works and others far more illiberal surely count as satire.

Charlie Hebdo, on the face of it, presented a case about freedom of the press and the criminality of mass killing. The murdered cartoonists deserved pity because they were murdered. The killers deserved to be hunted down, and their actions condemned, because killing is wrong. But in the shadow of the Rushdie fatwa and European anxiety prompted by impotence in the face of Salafist jihadism, the praise given to the magazine was soon assimilated to the dignity of the arts and letters in the war against terror. Once again, the wildness of satire was turned into an object of moral admiration. The cartoons were broad-gauge, and looked to get a rise out of the credulous—a very different thing from Rushdie's tactics of ambiguity and metafiction; coming from non-Muslim French artists, they made a conspicuous instance of satire from high to low. The watchwords of solidarity, "Je suis Charlie," could be repeated by state officials in France, Britain, and the US who regularly censored reports of drone killings in Pakistan and Yemen.

Here is a thought experiment. What would be the Western reaction to a cartoonist who leaned heavily on the most flagrant anti-Catholic or anti-Jewish clichés—Jesuits in cowl and robe conspiring to set a Catholic king on the English throne, or Jews drinking the blood of a Christian child? The anti-Catholic swipe would be looked on as a bizarre eccentricity, of no controversial interest at all; the anti-Jewish one might prompt alarm as a symptom of cultural regression; but in either case, ascription of moral courage and artistic merit would be out of the question. This may suggest why the defense of *Charlie Hebdo* as an equal-opportunity offender was misjudged. The cartoons were published at a time when a few Muslims were known to be terrorists and many others were outsiders in European society, exposed to prejudice of a kind no longer suffered by Christians or Jews. Complacency was a recurrent flaw in the European and North American praise of the cartoons. There is, after all, a difference between ridicule of the established and mockery of the unestablished. Though the difference can never rightly be reflected in laws, since laws must apply to everyone in the same way, *Charlie Hebdo* might have served to bring the matter to consciousness. But as with the September 11 attacks, the enormity of the crime and its spectacular quality combined to prevent thought. Accordingly, it was possible on January 11, 2015 for François Hollande, Angela Merkel, David Cameron, Benjamin Netanyahu, and three dozen world leaders to assemble shoulder to shoulder at the place de la République, to march twenty abreast with arms interlinked and to chant with the crowd of a million: "Je suis Charlie."

A sequel in a lower strain occurred soon afterward, with the announcement by PEN America that their Freedom of Expression Courage prize for 2015 would be awarded to *Charlie Hebdo*. By that time, a number of American writers and artists had come to share a certain tacit ambivalence about the cartoons. The prize was to be given partly in recognition of the physical courage required to publish a magazine as provocative as *Charlie Hebdo*; and there could be no doubt that its editors, writers, and illustrators exemplified such courage. But the PEN award was also meant to honor the moral courage of the magazine as a stimulus to public debate. These distinct criteria were collapsed together by the timing of the announcement and the name of the prize itself. In the event, more than 200 members of PEN signed a letter declaring their intention to boycott the literary gala at which the award was to be presented. In a separate and personal dissent, Deborah Eisenberg asked why French satirists of Islam were being singled out for honors when the US had plenty of home-grown satirists among the membership of college fraternities: "We are PEN America after all, not PEN France, and the fraternity brothers have expressed their views—even in humorous (to them) song—with great clarity and force."[4] The executive director of the PEN American Center, Suzanne Nossel, defended the decision in the high-minded spirit of Rushdie on liberty and truth. *Charlie Hebdo* stood "firmly within the tradition of French satire." It mocked religions but it also mocked "prejudices against religion, racial prejudices, ethnocentric attitudes and a whole range of other targets. . . . They defined their role as pushing boundaries, questioning orthodoxy, casting light on obscured motives and ensuring that nothing was above comment or debate."[5] Thus, the broad-church liberal and multicultural defense of *Charlie Hebdo* repeated the confusion of Hitchens in his "genuine,

devotional" brief for *The Satanic Verses* and of Rushdie in his defense of
the moral dignity of satire as such. The obligation to support the
censored and the persecuted was made to coincide with aesthetic
approval of their works and praise for their political acumen.

*   *   *

The Rushdie and *Charlie Hebdo* controversies both exemplify a pattern
of affirmation and denial. The commercial democracies in the West
have come to be of two minds about free speech. This condition is
ratified continually and remains hidden in plain view; one can feel by
now that the pattern almost defies introspection and cure. Freedom is
the international face we prepare to meet the faces that we meet—and
on that stage the great principle is often restated. The vainglory of
adopting free speech as a banner-slogan is recognized, but the temptation to strut is not altogether avoided. And yet in our private
conduct, and especially in educational institutions where the manners
of public debate are learned, the ethic of free speech has taken a very
different turn. People know that their words are monitored, beyond
their power to calibrate, and the respectable are more cautious than
ever before. They take great care not to speak bluntly. In America, the
mainstream media follow the protocol of a "balance" of views, according to which two sides must be offered in the discussion of any public
question, and control is ceded to a moderator whose questions obey a
mindless decorum: "Congressman X, what is your reaction to what
Senator Y just said?" In the small change of conversation, in the corpor-
ate, professional or academic milieu, a remark signaling strong disagreement is taken to be an impoliteness. The first article of workplace
wisdom is that any gesture or word that might cause friction is "unhelpful."

   In this new regime of manners, it is impossible to overrate the part
played by the soft despotism of social media. Our verbal surround-
ings online are created by affinity; and each day a hundred small
choices close the circle more tightly. You don't say wrong things—
the sort of things that will startle your friends. Or rather, your friends
by definition are the people who won't be startled by anything you
are likely to say. What are the implications for free speech? Double-
think, Orwell wrote apropos of life in Oceania, was the mental
technique that allowed one to "hold simultaneously two opinions
which cancelled out, knowing them to be contradictory and believing

in both of them." The process found its consummation in "the ultimate subtlety: consciously to induce unconsciousness, and then, once again, to become unconscious of the act of hypnosis you had just performed. Even to understand the word 'doublethink' involved the use of double-think." It is like that with freedom of speech and self-censorship in the West. We must spread freedom of speech in order to make the world free. And to do the job well, we must watch what we say.

When the Snowden revelations appeared in June 2013, a few observers compared the system they exposed—the data storage that could potentially be used against anyone—with the practice of the Stasi in East Germany. Liberal technocrats thought the analogy absurdly stretched. It was German, Eastern European, and Russian immigrants living in Europe and the US who vouched for the parallel. Yet Snowden's discoveries focused attention narrowly on the danger of surveillance by the government. From the prevalence and practices of social media, meanwhile, the groundwork had been laid to recruit a voluntary corps of citizen police. Their work is to listen for offensive things said in private, and to expose the offence by transferring the blamable words to the public realm. As these people see it (and they constitute a nameless civilian corps of thousands), *surveillance* promotes *safety* for the sake of *community*. They are believers in what Timothy Garton Ash calls "a connected world."

Garton Ash is a classical liberal with hopes for the attainment of a culture of international tolerance and freedom. His book *Free Speech: Ten Principles for a Connected World* has a good deal to say in passing about surveillance, safety, and community;[6] he can see the danger implicit in the assumption by the citizen police that exposure is knowledge and knowledge is freedom. But Garton Ash conciliates even as he criticizes the emergent morale. Surveillance, he thinks, has gone too far, but it is a good thing to the extent that it ensures safety; community may be coercive in its demands on individual citizens, yet greater mutual concern may lead to a better informed basis for empathy. An optimistic ground tone is preserved throughout: the multiplication of our connections will support the plurality of our truths. Garton Ash has apparently heard (but isn't much struck by) the argument that the actually existing internet isolates users in sectarian hives that become repositories of half-truth and propaganda: a home away from home for questionable opinions that never get debated.

To promote free inquiry into the present state of the argument, he has created his own site, freespeechdebate.com.

The rhetorical measure and coolness of *Free Speech* are meant to model a style of debate that could never erupt in acrimony; but an enforced equability has its own drawbacks. Garton Ash sees nothing but improvement in the fact that the internet "makes it easier to give people the choice of not looking if they don't want to"; so, "on freespeechdebate.com, we have adopted the one-click-away principle":[7] the site gives adequate warning of a disagreeable image coming soon, and it is then on the user to click or not to click. That is a lame alternative, unlikely to be much comfort to the angry and susceptible, and the proposal betrays a surprising innocence concerning the addictive properties of images. Plato's allegory of the cave needs very little revision to yield a warning about the lights and shadows on your laptop or iPad. Each click and stop is chosen, you may say, but it is also led on by a seduction that assists the choice. Garton Ash seems not to have recognized that words on the internet are often experienced as images, fleeting shadows whose signature has vanished. "I read somewhere online it said . . . ". This kind of abortive memory and disclaimer was seldom heard among the educated before the advent of web surfing.

In his overall argument, Garton Ash defends the maximum practicable tolerance, allowing only rare emergency exceptions. He also observes the distinction between "laws" and "norms" that has been much developed in the last two decades by Anglo-American philosophers and policy strategists. It is a useful distinction, but vulnerable to opportunistic abuse, as when President Obama deplored the violation of "international norms" to justify an armed intervention in Syria that was forbidden by international law. Garton Ash tells us that we should "maintain strict, consistent legal enforcement for clear harms, but mobilise the republic of norms for the rest."[8] The republic of norms is another name—it hasn't caught on yet—for the common sympathies that Hume called "the party of humanity." It played an important role in Hume's argument for the authority of reflective feelings and the civilizing of debate. We don't have to punish an infraction: we can always disapprove. In America, a litigious society since its founding, one of the unhappiest developments of the past two generations has been the loss of confidence in the power of disapproval. The fear is that disapproval won't suffice until you press your claim to the point of litigation and a threat of punishment—a change that was already far along before the internet made things worse.

A liberal belief in the utility of norms may also have been weakened by one feature of the pluralism of Isaiah Berlin—a thinker whose work has done much to shape Garton Ash's understanding of freedom. Berlin sought to apply an idea of political tolerance not only to persons but to whole cultures; the reason was that cultures themselves were expressive achievements akin to works of art. It is evident how such an argument, though classical-liberal in its origins, might flower in a defense of identity politics; and in the US and Britain, its influence has certainly been to discourage criticism of identity politics. If cultures resemble works of art, if they are supposed to speak in different languages that resist translation, how can my norms be governed by yours? And more: given the investment each person must have in a cultural identity, how can disapproval ever be enough to meet the offence of seeing one's identity harmed by insult?

Addressing the expanded field for taking offence which is visible any day on the internet and promoted by the identity cultures, Garton Ash is at his most moderate and unsatisfactory. He can see the sense of "trigger warnings," but thinks they should be confined to occasions "when something could genuinely trigger trauma." But why be so elastic? Trauma has a rigorous clinical definition that could have been cited against the mock-clinical warnings. He treats the advocacy scholarship in this area with a studied politeness, but the protocol that requires a teacher to pull a long face is spreading. A letter to the *New York Times* on July 31, 2015, from an administrator in the city's Education Department, denounces a reading-skills exam that used an extract from Edith Wharton's *Age of Innocence*; the passage in question begins, "It was generally agreed in New York that the Countess Olenska had 'lost her looks'"; the complaint is that "any girl taking the exam" will experience the mention of losing your looks as a "psychic punch" that impairs concentration on the rest of the exam.

* * *

"It is time to explain myself," Whitman says in Part 44 of *Song of Myself*; this essay is far along, and it is time. The difficulties of legislation on speech have grown more complex with the elaboration of other rights, but in some ways we have never simplified enough. The freedom to speak one's mind is a physical necessity, not a political and intellectual piece of good luck; to a thinking person, the need seems to be almost as natural as breathing. "How do I know what I think till I see what I say?" The question applies not just to writing but to friendly or unfriendly conversation, or a muttered soliloquy. Yet the good of free speech has seldom been a common intuition, and it is not a universal experience. It matters to a few, much of the time, and to others at unpredictable times. Dissident minorities took the clearest advantage of this liberty in the high age of Protestant dissent and political radicalism—roughly the three and a half centuries from the onset of the Puritan revolution in England to the height of the Solidarity protests in Poland.

The heroic picture of the individual heretic standing against the Church, the dissenter against the state, the artist against the mass culture, has been fading for a while, and we have not yet found anything to put in its place. Asked in a late interview how he fell away from his belief in Catholic doctrine, Graham Greene said he had been converted by arguments and he had forgotten the arguments. Something like this has happened to left liberals where freedom of speech is concerned. The last two generations were brought to see its value by arguments, and they have forgotten the arguments. Few have felt oppressed by the rigors of censorship; more have been interested in censoring harmful speech by politicians or members of the "dominant culture" (which includes white people of humble means). Taking note of the recent protests that forced the "disinviting" of commencement speakers at Brown, Johns Hopkins, Williams, and Haverford, the censorious monitoring at Brandeis University of a teacher who said that Mexican laborers were once called "wetbacks," and many similar incidents starting in 2013, the sociologist Jonathan Cole pointed out in the *Atlantic* that the students at these elite establishments, including the most vigilant of the speech monitors, have followed all their lives "a straight and narrow path." They have never deviated into "a passion unrelated to school work, and have not been allowed, therefore, to live what many would consider a normal childhood—to play, to learn by doing, to challenge their teachers, to make mistakes."[9] They have always been on good behavior; and they don't regret it. They are therefore ill-equipped to defend anything the authorities or their activist classmates tell them should count as bad behavior. These people have grown up, Cole adds, in the years since 2001 when the schools and the popular culture, in America above all, kept up an incessant drone about personal safety, the danger of terrorist attacks, and the opacity of every culture to every other culture. It is a generation in which the word "fragile" is routinely applied to daily shifts of mood.

Few of them have had the experience of being a minority of one, or a little more than one. Admittedly most people have never been in that situation (including, perhaps, most of the people one might call good). But a new keenness of censorious distrust has come from a built-in suspicion of the outliers in public discussion. Social media refer to these people as "trolls" and sometimes as "stalkers"; any flicker of curiosity about their ideas is pre-empted by a question that is not a question: "What's *wrong* with them?" Meanwhile, those inside a given group have their settled audience of friends and followers, to adopt the revealing jargon of Facebook and Twitter: a self-sufficient collectivity and happy to stay that way. To be "friended" in the Facebook world is to be safe—walled-up and wadded-in by chosen and familiar connections. An unsafe space is a space where, if they knew you were there, they might unfriend you. As Sherry Turkle puts it in *Reclaiming Conversation*, a penetrating study of the change of manners brought about by social media: "If you grew up in the world of 'I share, therefore I am,' you may not have confidence that you have a thought unless you are sharing it." And it is a full-time regime for the young. "Most are already sleeping with their phones," Turkle says of the children and teenagers she interviewed. "So, if they wake up in the middle of the night, they check their messages."[10] But these are messages sent and received within the group; outside, all is uncertain, obscure, and apt to bring on sensations of fragility. Adversarial stimuli are to be ignored where possible and prohibited where necessary.

Within such a group, spontaneous speech—unconditioned by the context of sharing and the previous expectations of the group—is nothing like a physical need. The very idea of membership, of affinity and loyalty, reduces the likelihood of an infraction that could carry an unpleasant surprise. Where Facebook has a thumbs-up symbol—meaning "I like this and kind of agree!"—but no thumbs-down, who will risk an exorbitant word? The cost would be a forced exit from the group; and the group is the lungs that make speech possible.

A provocative and half-disagreeable remark amounts to a declaration of the intention to defect. To someone who has grown up in such a setting, the older protections of individual speech are an irrelevance.

A few days before Halloween 2015, a diversity administrator at Yale University sent around a notice advising students to mind that their costumes didn't cause offence or encroach on sensibilities of gender, race, or culture. The associate master of a residential college responded with an email addressed to the students in her college, saying that Halloween was a time for a lark and everyone should lighten up. Even a decade ago, both the cautionary letter and the reply would have seemed hilarious for their condescension and paternalism. In the present climate, it was the reply that led to an immediate demand by some residents of the college that the associate master be sacked (and with her the master, her husband, who had failed to keep her in line). An undergraduate writing with much emotion in a student newspaper testified that the permission granted to culturally appropriative and possibly insulting costumes had deprived her of a safe space; after reading the wretched email, she found herself unable to eat, sleep, or do homework in a building where authority had been ceded to the person who wrote it. From the point of view of her group, this student was speaking common sense. Who would want to smash a formed consensus for inoffensive costumes? On the same Halloween of 2015, at Claremont McKenna College in Southern California, photos of two female students dressed in sombreros, ponchos, and moustaches set off a protest march of thousands, including activists from neighboring campuses, and the scandal prompted the dean of the college to resign.

Scenes of mass emotion are becoming more common in our time. Such scenes are by nature congenial to the impulse of censorship. The outbreaks of punitive certitude in the US, from Tea Party rallies to the anti-Halloween rallies on campus, nonetheless are difficult to account for in detail. C. Wright Mills drew a distinction between "the personal troubles of milieu" and "the public issues of social structure" that seems pertinent here. If the expectations and exclusions of every milieu are added up, in the hope that this will lead to a grasp of relevant truths about social structure, honest debate in public will become a thing of the past. It requires considerable patience and learning to criticize an unjust social structure. By contrast, our own milieu is what we know, and social media tell us we are right to shield ourselves from particles foreign to the milieu. For many people today, an identity culture or identity politics may seem a necessary shelter from the tidal force of the mass culture. It affords a place for "affirmation" and "resilience"; and yet its immediate purpose is largely negative and protective. To those who seek and find validation in this way, it is natural to embrace a form of censorship. The contraction goes with the situation.

* * *

What drove the early modern proponents of free speech to deny the legitimacy of any form of censorship? The heart of Milton's attack in *Areopagitica* lies in his refusal to claim innocence for any human activity. It is the presumption of innocence by the censor that most deeply informs the zeal for silencing opinions that are thought to be intolerable:

> Good and evil we know in the field of this world grow up together almost inseparably; and the knowledge of good is so involved and interwoven with the knowledge of evil, and in so many cunning resemblances hardly to be discerned, that those confused seeds which were imposed on Psyche as an incessant labor to cull out and sort asunder, were not more intermixed. It was from out the rind of one apple tasted, that the knowledge of good and evil, as two twins cleaving together, leaped forth into the world. And perhaps this is that doom which Adam fell into of knowing good and evil, that is to say, of knowing good by evil. . . . Assuredly we bring not innocence into the world, we bring impurity much rather: that which purifies us is trial, and trial is by what is contrary. That virtue therefore which is but a youngling in the contemplation of evil, and knows not the utmost that vice promises to her followers, and rejects it, is but a blank virtue, not a pure; her whiteness is but an excremental whiteness.[11]

To try to purify ourselves, by renouncing all exposure to dangerous words, is to legislate for the preservation of our innocence; but Milton doubts that this can be done. The censor holds a very different view: impurity invades or insinuates from outside, it is a kind of pollution, and the duty of moral guardians is to secure and deliver us. (It is understood that we ourselves have committed no trespass that needs to be forgiven.) Many people want to be protected against "trial by what is contrary": if others brush against them in a way they don't like, though no harm was done, they want to penalize what is contrary. But the benefits obtainable through censorship turn out to be delusive once we recognize that good and evil "grow up together almost inseparably." So Milton concludes that censorship cannot make us better. Impurity, after all, springs from us, among others. Any law devised to winnow out the noxious materials can only weaken the very people it protects.

We may seem on much lower ground if we look for help to a well-known argument in Mill's *On Liberty*. "The truth of an opinion," Mill says, "is part of its utility." He appears to mean that the gradual victory of truth over falsehood will depend on a freedom of debate that allows the clash of rival opinions: people sort out the useful truths from the useless falsehoods, and we support liberty of discussion from an instrumental motive, because we want society to grow ever more enlightened. This utilitarian justification asks us to prize truth for the sake of the improvement it will bring; but if there are experts on what exactly is useful and improving for the species, there seems to be no reason why we shouldn't silence people whose ignorance and obduracy will be a drag on progress. Yet the proposed connection between truth, utility, and free discussion is a secondary argument for Mill. The real antagonist of *On Liberty* is not intellectual backwardness. It is rather what Mill calls "our merely social intolerance": a form of tyranny possible to every person, which, if we obeyed its promptings, would become a lever for "intellectual pacification" and "the sacrifice of the entire moral courage of the human mind."

The possession of such moral courage has nothing to do with measurements of utility, as Mill makes clear in an uncompromising passage:

> Let us suppose ... that the government is entirely at one with the people, and never thinks of exerting any power of coercion [to restrict the liberty of thought and discussion] unless in agreement with what it conceives to be their voice. But I deny the right of the people to exercise such coercion, either by themselves or by their government. The power itself is illegitimate. The best government has no more title to it than the worst. It is as noxious, or more noxious, when exerted in accordance with public opinion, than when in opposition to it. If all mankind minus one, were of one opinion, and only one person were of the contrary opinion, mankind would be no more justified in silencing that one

person, than he, if he had the power, would be justified in silencing mankind.[12]

Quote this passage to a roomful of academics today, withhold the name of Mill, and not one in three will credit that any intelligent person could ever think something so improbable. If the "power of coercion" is taken to mean a painful use of force, *that*, they will agree, is bad. But by "coercion" Mill also means the affixing of any penalty at all to dissent from what the majority supposes are the components of a better world. "The power itself is illegitimate." Mill speaks here neither for truth nor for utility, and gives value to something separate: the right of the person who wants to speak not to be silenced. This insight of *On Liberty* is consonant with the Mill of *The Subjection of Women* rather than *Utilitarianism*. There are things that are owing to persons, he believes, simply because they are persons. Freedom from subordination because of one's sex or sect is an irreducible good. So is the freedom to know your mind by speaking your mind to another person. Mill hates pacification more than he loves progress. His own brief comment makes the best gloss on the passage: "Not the violent conflict between parts of the truth, but the quiet suppression of half of it, is the formidable evil."

Regarding the pressure for restraint on speech that might arouse strong emotions, Mill notices that interested opponents may always join forces with a pacified majority to exclude a detested person from speaking on grounds of manners. In a society that professes to defend free speech, the preferred tactic will be to rule the person out of bounds because of the extreme character and vehemence of his words:

> Much might be said on the impossibility of fixing where these supposed bounds are to be placed; for if the test be offence to those whose opinion is attacked, I think experience testifies that this offence is given whenever the attack is telling and powerful, and that every opponent who pushes them hard, and whom they find it difficult to answer, appears to them, if he shows any strong feeling on the subject, an intemperate opponent.[13]

Scruples about the dividing line between proper and intemperate speech receive a far less skeptical treatment today in most American colleges and universities. The watchword here is "civility." It cropped up two years ago, where one might not expect it, in a celebration of the fiftieth anniversary of the Berkeley Free Speech Movement.

* * *

The protest of 1964 was about liberty of discussion, in the plainest possible sense of both words. The University of California administration had closed down part of the campus that civil rights workers used to speak, distribute literature, and draw students into the movement. Protesters saw this as an act of arbitrary power in the interest of restricting opinion, and they asked for unrestricted free speech. The climax came with Mario Savio's speech on the steps of Sproul Hall, an utterance that was principled, persuasive, extraordinary both in its passion and its reserve. Having just returned from a meeting with an administrator, he reported the upshot:

> We have an autocracy which runs this university. It's managed! We asked, if President Kerr actually tried to get something more liberal out of the Regents in his telephone conversation, why didn't he make some public statement to that effect? And the answer we received, from a well-meaning liberal, was the following. He said: "Would you ever imagine the manager of a firm making a statement publicly in opposition to his board of directors?" That's the answer. Now I ask you to consider: if this is a firm—and if the Board of Regents are the board of directors—and if President Kerr in fact is the manager—then I'll tell you something: the faculty are a bunch of employees and we're the raw materials! But we're a bunch of raw materials that don't mean to have any process upon us; don't mean to be made into any product; don't mean to end up being bought by some clients of the university, be they the government, be they industry, be they organized labor, be they anyone. We're human beings! . . . There's a time when the operation of the machine becomes so odious, makes you so sick at heart that you can't take part, you can't even passively take part. And you've got to put your bodies upon the gears and upon the wheels, upon the levers, upon all the apparatus, and you've got to make it stop! And you've got to indicate to the people who run it, to the people who own it, that unless you're free the machine will be prevented from working at all! . . . That doesn't mean—and it will be interpreted to mean, unfortunately, by the bigots who run the [*San Francisco*] *Examiner*—that you have to break anything. One thousand people sitting down some place, not letting anybody by, not letting anything happen, can stop any machine, including this machine, and it will stop![14]

The whole speech can be heard online, and it is his voice that carries the passion and conviction—by no means a polished or disciplined public voice. Savio was an undergraduate philosophy major (a few days short of 22) who had already participated in the Mississippi Freedom Summer, and his delivery leaves no doubt of his "strong feeling on the subject"—climbing to a pitch of ferocity before calming himself, and the audience too, with his words about the non-violent tactics that would do no harm to innocent persons or the fame of the cause.

In 1964 the aim of the protests had been to remove the last barriers on unrestricted speech. Savio was always explicit about this. Fifty years later, the chancellor of UC Berkeley, Nicholas Dirks, sent a public letter to faculty, students, and staff advising how best to honor the spirit of the Free Speech Movement. They should always remember that they live in a diversely constituted "community" where a standard of "respect" was a precondition of "safe" use of the privilege of free speech. Above all, they must take care not to speak with unseemly passion:

> When issues are inherently divisive, controversial and capable of arousing strong feelings, the commitment to free speech and expression can lead to division and divisiveness that undermine a community's foundation.... We can only exercise our right to free speech insofar as we feel safe and respected in doing so, and this in turn requires that people treat each other with civility. Simply put, courteousness and respect in words and deeds are basic preconditions to any meaningful exchange of ideas. In this sense, free speech and civility are two sides of a single coin—the coin of open, democratic society.[15]

Reduced to a practical directive, the first sentence says: "Indulge in free speech if you must; but please avoid issues that are controversial; and if you do address such issues, don't sound as if you care about them intensely." This is what Mill meant by quiet suppression.

Two contradictory thoughts now dominate the Anglo-American approach to feelings in the context of public debate. For the speaker, feelings must be restrained—a neutral style of rational euphemism is recommended. On the other hand, the emotion felt by the listener in response to a speech must be treated as authoritative, unarguable, closed to correction or modification by other witnesses. "The group which feels hurt is the ultimate arbiter of whether a hurt has taken place"; so, too, the person who listens and testifies on behalf of his or her group. Reproach from a traumatized listener admits of no answer, only apology, even though apologies are only interesting in proportion as they are spontaneous and warranted. The apology that is demanded and forked out has the moral stature of hush money: it makes a fetish of insincerity. With some help from the jargon of political and religious heresy, one would say these are not so much apologies as formal acts of *self-criticism* and *recantation*. Thus far, they have mostly been extorted in communities the size of a guild or a college. At the same time the rigor of exclusion within these mini-communities is itself a cause of the near-autistic breakdown of political speech in America.

* * *

The deeper distortions of mass psychology show up first in peculiar tics and involutions of language—the relation is that of symptom to anxiety. In 2003 the United States bombed, invaded, and occupied Iraq, and set the Middle East on fire. The event is generally talked of as a "mistake." But there was a legal name for it, "a war of aggression," and in the past several years in America, colleges and other small communities have witnessed the discovery of a new crime: the microaggression. From a certain distance, the concept of the microaggression has the quality of a repressed memory, a recognition of violence elsewhere that surfaces in denial and displacement. A microaggression occurs typically if, in an encounter between a white and a black person, or between a member of the "dominant culture" and anyone not identified with that culture, the former by word or gesture betrays an assumption that there is something unusual about the latter. Invidious attention is thereby called to an unspoken but glaring fact of inequality, and the dominant assumption is laid bare. This can happen in an awkward motion that is embarrassing but possibly not ill-meant—an 18-year-old white undergraduate asking an 18-year-old black if she can touch her hair. An example often cited is the laying on the non-dominant person the burden to testify about her experience from her special place in a spectrum of diversity. Any word or gesture that is taken to imply such singling out is a microaggression if the person addressed thinks that it is. This makes for a double bind: a white student passing a black and not looking at him could plausibly be charged with microaggression. Replay the same encounter, but with an unusually long look—say, five or six seconds—and the charge of microaggression is just as plausible.

How should the infraction be punished? By re-education, it has been suggested, in the form of additional diversity training and sensitivity training. Persuaded by this concept and by a therapeutic literature and practice that cater to it, young people of more than one race have come to think themselves uniquely delicate and exposed. The counterpart of the microaggression is the microtrauma which makes up in nearness and frequency what it lacks in intensity and duration. Here again one is struck by the action of displacement. The three American presidents since 2001 have said over and over that their primary duty was "the safety of the American people." No earlier presidents spoke in quite this way: the oath of office contains not a word about safety but commits the chief magistrate to uphold the constitution. Safety in argument or debate is of course an unintelligible demand, but the trouble with those who think they want it isn't that they are incapable of giving reasons backed by evidence. Rather, they have had no practice in using words to influence people unlike themselves. That is an art that can be lost. It depends on a quantum of accidental communication that is missing in a life of organized contacts.

"Debate is not a death sentence," Beatrix Campbell recently observed, "and feeling offended is not the same as feeling or being exterminated. There is a human right to life, but there is no right to be not offended."[16] The truth is that in some areas we are close to excogitating a right not to feel offended. In America, the definitions governing what counts as sexual harassment are wide enough to have let in a troop of other causes. The ban on "unwanted approach" and irritants productive of a "hostile work environment" are easily extended from action to speech: the unwanted approach becomes unwelcome words, the hostile work environment a hostile speech environment. The words *right*, *feel*, and *offended*, in Campbell's sharp formulation, all are coming to have legal definitions that carry immediate force. It is a right because its violation exposes the offender to penalties of fine, imprisonment, or mandatory re-education. Feeling counts because feeling in the offended person is a dispositive fact: proof (which needs no further support) that a crime was committed. We are not far in America—is it just America?—from evolving a right to feel good about ourselves. Possibly the best counteraction is to repudiate membership in a species that could want to do this. Misanthropy and the rejection of censorship here join forces unambiguously.

What a distinguished and very dead philosopher referred to as the religion of humanity may turn out to be as dangerous as all the other religions. With the joint arrival of multicultural etiquette and globalization, we have come to dwell increasingly on hidden injuries that threaten the norms and civilities desirable for people everywhere. This involves a fresh dedication to the discovery of faults of manners and usage that could cause friction. But, as was observed half a century ago by Nigel Dennis—an irreplaceable satirist of political and religious fanaticism—"Our sins are rarely as disgusting as we suppose them to be, and never as disgusting as the attention we pay them."[17] Nor do we know ourselves well enough to be sure that our corrections are correct. The narcissism of humanity remains as conspicuous as ever at a moment when we can least afford the indulgence.

Government by consent of the governed is on trial; events in Britain and America in the years since 2015 prove it with irrefutable clarity. But if government by consent can be made to work, its fortunes will depend on a good many people being inquisitive and hardened against the officious numbering of infractions—a tactic that is often cowardly and never a substitute for counter-speech. Reports of bodily harm at the enunciation of unpleasant words, and of clinical depression from exposure to despised historical names in public places, suggest a delicacy that would render politics eventually impossible. The wrongs of the past, as well as of the present, ought to be redressed in a medium more solid than language; but speech has always been as mixed, as improper, as dirty as action; and unhappily even the cure is bound to carry traces of the impurity of the physician. Whatever led us to expect innocence from people like us?

Notes

Chapter 1

1. *The Poems of John Milton*, ed. John Carey and Alastair Fowler (London, 1968), pp. 411–12. All subsequent quotations of Milton's poetry are from this edition.
2. *The Poems of Tennyson*, ed. Christopher Ricks (New York, 1972), p. 1320.
3. Edmund Burke, *Writings and Speeches*, 9 vols (Oxford, 1981–2015), vol. 5, p. 403.
4. Edmund Burke, *The Correspondence of Edmund Burke*, 10 vols (Cambridge, 1958–78), vol. 6, p. 40.
5. G. Lowes Dickinson, *The Greek View of Life* (New York, 1911), pp. 218–19.
6. Aristophanes, *Four Plays*, trans. Dudley Fitts (New York, 1962), p. 145.
7. Bryan Garsten, *Saving Persuasion* (Cambridge, Mass., 2006), p. 135.
8. J. L. Austin, *Philosophical Essays* (Oxford, 1961), p. 226.
9. Ibid. 226.
10. Ibid. 231.
11. Ibid. 223.
12. Ibid. 130.
13. Ibid. 149.
14. Ibid. 150.
15. Donald Davidson, *Truth, Language, and History* (Oxford, 2005), pp. 98–9.
16. Plato, *Phaedrus*, trans. W. C. Helmbold and W. G. Rabinowitz (Indianapolis, 1956), pp. 69–70.
17. Cicero, *De Oratore*, Books 1 and 2, trans. E. W. Sutton and H. Rackham (Cambridge, Mass., 1948), pp. 89–91.
18. Ibid. 161.
19. Ibid. 161.
20. Ibid. 337.
21. Cicero, *The Verrine Orations*, trans. L. H. G. Greenwood (Cambridge, Mass., 1928), p. 233.

Chapter 2

1. *Julius Caesar*, ed. David Daniell (London, 1998), I.ii.210–11. All subsequent quotations are from this edition.
2. *Brecht on Theatre*, ed. and trans. John Willett (New York, 1964), p. 137.
3. *Measure for Measure*, ed. J. W. Lever (Walton-on-Thames, 1998), II.ii.162.
4. *Poems of Milton*, p. 467.
5. Ibid. 468.

6. William Empson, *Milton's God* (London, 1961), pp. 27–8.

7. Henry James, *The Portrait of a Lady* (Oxford, 1981), pp. 442–3. All subsequent references are to this edition.

8. George Herbert Mead, "The Social Self," in *Selected Writings* (Chicago, 1981), p. 137.

9. Iris Murdoch, "The Sublime and the Beautiful Revisited," in *Existentialists and Mystics*, ed. Peter Conradi (New York, 1997), p. 281.

10. *The Portrait of a Lady*, pp. 461–2.

11. William James, *Pragmatism* (lecture VIII), in *Pragmatism and The Meaning of Truth* (Cambridge, Mass., 1978), p. 135.

Chapter 3

1. Adam Smith, *The Theory of Moral Sentiments* (Oxford, 1979), III.3.4.

2. Burke, *Writings and Speeches*, vol. 3, pp. 648–9.

3. Ibid. vol. 5, p. 477.

4. Richard Bourke, *Empire and Revolution* (Princeton, NJ: 2015), p. 568.

5. *Works of Edmund Burke*, 12 vols (Boston, Mass.: 1869), vol. 9, pp. 454–8.

6. See Frederick G. Whelan, *Edmund Burke and India* (Pittsburgh, Penn.: 1996), pp. 19–25; P. J. Marshall, *The Making and Unmaking of Empires* (Oxford, 2005), pp. 378–9.

7. *The Works and Life of Walter Bagehot*, ed. Mrs. Russell Barrington, 10 vols (London, 1915), vol. 5, p. 102.

8. Ibid. 109–10.

9. F. H. Bradley, *Ethical Studies* (London, 1876), p. 156.

10. Abraham Lincoln, *Speeches and Writings 1852–1858*, ed. Don Fehrenbacher (New York, 1989), p. 346.

11. Ibid. 346–7.

12. Ibid. 426.

13. Kenneth Burke, *A Rhetoric of Motives* (Berkeley, 1969), p. 50.

14. See Don Fehrenbacher, *Prelude to Greatness* (Stanford, Calif.: 1962), pp. 70–95.

15. Abraham Lincoln, *Speeches and Writings 1859–1865*, ed. Don Fehrenbacher (New York, 1989), p. 128.

Chapter 4

1. W. B. Yeats, *Collected Poems* (New York, 1956), p. 240. All subsequent quotations are from this edition.

2. See Stendhal, *Love*, trans. Gilbert and Suzanne Sale (London, 1957), section 133: "The greatest flattery that the most frenzied imagination could invent, to describe the generation growing up amongst us to take possession of life, opinion, and power, turns out to be a truth clearer than delight. The new generation has nothing to *continue* but everything to *create*. The great merit of Napoleon is that *he made a clean sweep.*"

3. W. B. Yeats, *Explorations* (New York, 1963), pp. 425–6. Ellipsis in original.

4. Ibid. 434.

5. George Orwell, *Collected Essays, Journalism, and Letters*, 4 vols (New York, 1968), p. 271.

6. Ibid., p. 273. Conor Cruise O'Brien, *Passion and Cunning* (New York, 1988), pp. 8–61, pursued the same intimation convincingly in a full-scale interpretation.

7. Orwell, *Collected Essays*, p. 274.

8. Ibid. 276.

9. W. H. Auden, *Spain* (London, 1937). All subsequent quotations are from this edition.

10. Orwell, *Collected Essays*, vol. 1, p. 516.

11. In an otherwise appreciative review of *Another Time* (the volume in which Auden's elegy was first reprinted), William Empson noticed this easy intimacy as a questionable trait: "you are afraid on every page that a horrid false note of infantilism will poke up its head. The poems here about famous men give striking cases of it"; see Empson, *Argufying*, ed. John Haffenden (Iowa City, 1987), p. 372.

12. Edward Mendelson, ed., *The English Auden* (New York, 1977), p. 390.

13. Edward Mendelson, *Later Auden* (New York, 1999), p. 17.

14. *The English Auden*, p. 393.

Chapter 5

1. Leonard W. Levy, *Blasphemy* (New York, 1993), p. 579.

2. Syed Shahabuddin, "You Did This with Satanic Forethought, Mr Rushdie," in *The Rushdie File*, ed. Lisa Appignanesi and Sara Maitland (London, 1990), p. 40; Immanuel Jakobovits, letter to *The Times*, March 4, 1989; Tariq Modood, "Religious Anger and Minority Rights," *Political Quarterly* (July 1989), p. 284.

3. Salman Rushdie, statement posted by English PEN, January 7, 2015: https://www.englishpen.org/campaigns/salman-rushdie-condemns-attack-on-charlie-hebdo/

4. Quoted by Glenn Greenwald, "Letters and Comments of PEN Writers Protesting the Charlie Hebdo Award," *The Intercept*, April 27, 2015.

5. Ibid.

6. Timothy Garton Ash, *Free Speech: Ten Principles for a Connected World* (New Haven, 2016).

7. Ibid. 126.

8. Ibid. 187.

9. Jonathan Cole, "The Chilling Effect of Fear at America's Colleges," *The Atlantic* online, June 9, 2016.

10. Sherry Turkle, *Reclaiming Conversation* (New York, 2015), pp. 66, 287.

11. John Milton, *Complete Poems and Major Prose*, ed. Merritt Y. Hughes (Indianapolis, 1957), p. 728.

12. John Stuart Mill, *On Liberty*, ed. David Bromwich and George Kateb (New Haven, 2003), p. 87.
13. Ibid. 118.
14. *The Essential Mario Savio*, ed. Robert Cohen (Berkeley, 2014), pp. 187–8; punctuation mine.
15. Quoted in *The Berkeley Daily Planet*, September 11, 2014.
16. Beatrix Campbell, *London Review of Books*, July 14, 2016.
17. Nigel Dennis, *Two Plays and a Preface* (New York, 1958), p. 51.

Index